"For a new generation of builders, this is your Think and Grow Rich." —Marcus Sheridan

BURN THE PLAYBOOK

Are You Made for More?
Build a Life on Your Terms.

BY JOE PULIZZI

BURN THE PLAYBOOK

ARE YOU MADE FOR MORE?

BUILD A LIFE ON YOUR TERMS.

JOE PULIZZI

For entrepreneurs and those stuck in a job that brings no satisfaction:
The system was never built for your freedom. Burn it. Build your own.
This isn't a book. It's a match. Light it.

"Joe Pulizzi has written the manifesto every frustrated employee and aspiring entrepreneur needs. Stop playing someone else's game and start building something that truly matters."

—Ann Handley, *Wall Street Journal* bestselling author of *Everybody Writes*

"Job security is a thing of the past. The only job security is getting comfortable with charting your own path, and this book shows you how it's done."

—Jay Clouse, founder, Creator Science

"Part strategy, part therapy, part kick in the ass. You'll thank yourself for reading this."

—Alexis Grant, creator and founder, They Got Acquired

"Most authors portray success as paint-by-numbers, but Joe resonates deeper. He knows how to navigate the calling of creators: the blank canvas."

—Jay Acunzo, author of *Break the Wheel: Question Best Practices, Trust Your Intuition, Do Your Best Work*

"Burn the Playbook should come with asbestos gloves. It's that hot!"

—Jay Baer, *New York Times* bestselling author and Hall of Fame speaker

You weren't born to follow rules. You were built to rewrite them.

ISBN: 979-8-9992878-2-3

Tilt Publishing
700 Park Offices Drive, Suite 250
Research Triangle, NC 27709

For my children.

Inspired by the love of my life.

Phil: 4:13

CONTENTS

You'll never be ready, but this chapter will help.

You don't need their playbook. You need your own.

Build momentum. One small win at a time.

INTRODUCTION

"How much to not live your life? How much to not follow your dreams?"

—*Jimmy Carr*

You've been sold a story about success: Work hard. Get good grades. Get a good job. Buy a house. Climb the ladder. Retire at 65. Live happily ever after.

That story *might* have worked once. It rarely works anymore.

We're living through one of the biggest shifts in how wealth, freedom, and meaning are created. The old playbook is broken . . . and the majority who follow it end up exhausted, frustrated, and stuck playing a game they can't win.

That's why this book exists.

Not to hand you another set of "rules."

Not to promise you an easy path.

But to help you **burn the outdated playbook** and **build a life that actually works**. On your terms.

WHY BURN THE PLAYBOOK?

In 1937, Napoleon Hill wrote *Think and Grow Rich*, a book that taught generations how to think differently about success. His ideas about belief, desire, and persistence have stood the test of time. And it made a deep and profound difference in my own life.

But the world has changed dramatically since then:

- We don't build factories anymore. We build audiences.
- We don't just compete for jobs. We create our own platforms.
- We don't measure success by titles. We measure it by freedom.

And while technology took the factory jobs, AI is now threatening the knowledge workers.

While Hill's core principles still matter, we need a new direction for this world. For people who want to matter more and build something real.

You're not here to fit in. You're here to create. To lead. To build a life you don't have to escape from.

WHAT'S THE GOAL?

What do you think of when you see the word "success"?

It's different for everyone.

To me, success means independence: the ability to build a life, family, and career on your terms. It means you are not controlled by other people, other companies, or other circumstances. It means you own all the decisions to make a life that positively impacts yourself and your family and helps to create a better world.

It also means service.

Dan Martell says, "Everything you want, sits on the other side of helping other people get it." The more people you help, the more doors open. For freedom, for opportunity, and for meaning. Success isn't about getting ahead; it's about lifting others as you go.

But that kind of success doesn't happen by accident. And it surely doesn't happen by following someone else's script.

The old playbook, where you go to school, get a stable job, work hard, retire at 65; it wasn't designed for freedom. It was designed for safety. Compliance. Predictability.

And today? It doesn't even guarantee *that*.

This book is about building something else. Something you own. A business. A system. A rhythm. A mindset.

Something that gives you leverage . . . financially, emotionally, and spiritually.

So what's the goal?

The goal is to give you the tools and mindset to *burn what's not working* and start creating something that is.

This isn't theory. It's a call to action. Not just to grow. But to grow free. Not to quit. But to *build*.

The goal is yours to define. But by the end of this book, you'll have a clear path to get there. On your terms.

"I see all this potential, and I see it squandered. God damn it, an entire generation pumping gas, waiting tables—slaves with white collars. Advertising has us chasing cars and clothes, working jobs we hate so we can buy shit we don't need. We're the middle children of history, man. No purpose or place. We have no Great War. No Great Depression. Our great war is a spiritual war. Our great depression is our lives. We've all been raised on television to believe that one day we'd all be millionaires, and movie gods, and rock stars, but we won't. We're slowly learning that fact. And we're very, very pissed off."

—Speech by Tyler Durden (Brad Pitt) in the movie *Fight Club*

WHO THIS BOOK IS FOR

If you fall into one of one of the three following groups, *Burn the Playbook* was written for you.

THE EMERGING CREATOR

You're in the early stages. Maybe you're building an audience on YouTube, TikTok, Instagram, or with your newsletter. But your revenue doesn't match your ambition. You're trying things, but the path still feels muddy. You know there's power in creating, but you haven't figured out how to turn content into a system and a system into freedom.

This book will help you connect the dots and give you the tools to build something you own.

THE POSTGRAD EXPLORER

You just finished high school or college. You did what they told you. And now? The traditional job path feels hollow. You want more . . . more flexibility, more ownership, more purpose. You're not afraid to work hard; you're just not willing to waste your life doing something meaningless.

This book will show you that there's another way . . . and exactly how to start building it from the ground up.

THE CAREER-TRAPPED MIDLIFE REBEL

You've spent years climbing someone else's ladder, and it's slowly killing you. You don't hate work. You hate not having control. You know you're capable of more, but the system doesn't care. You want out. But you don't just want to quit. You want a plan.

This book will help you shift your mindset from employee to owner and give you the steps to turn your knowledge into leverage.

And for each of you, here's the truth: **Whether you realize it or not, you're already a content creator.**

Every post, video, email, podcast, or DM is a signal. The question is, will you keep giving your energy to platforms that profit from your attention, or will you start building something you control?

Some will see the opportunity and act. Most will scroll past it.

But for those who commit? There's never been a better time to build freedom from the inside out.

Now, if you don't feel the call of content creation, this book will still help you. Any business in any industry is fueled by marketing, and there is no better marketing than building an audience that knows, likes, and trusts you. The easiest way to build a business today is audience first, product second. Please keep that in mind throughout the book.

HOW TO USE THIS BOOK

Burn the Playbook is simple by design.

Each chapter gives you a core principle to live by and a challenge to act on. You'll find comparisons to the old ways (**What Hill Said**) and the realities of today (**What It Means Now**). Short, clear, actionable. *I built this book like a feed: short bursts of content, each with a key point, every point building on a broader idea.*

This is a book you can come back to when you're stuck, overwhelmed, or just need a reminder: **You don't have to follow someone else's path. You can create your own.**

And it doesn't matter what age you are. I started at age 32 and continue this journey at 52. Wally Koval (*Accidentally Wes Anderson*) started in his late 20s. Julia McCoy (First Movers) was in her 30s. Robert Rose (Seventh Bear) was just beyond 40. Brian Piper (content optimization) was already 50. It's never too late to burn the playbook.

And this isn't about burning everything down out of anger. It's about burning down what no longer serves you so you can build what does.

Burn the playbook. Build what matters. On Your Terms. Whether you're 19 or 91, your future isn't written yet.

Time to start.

"Anything is possible. That's how I look at it. There's electricity. There are shooting stars. There's lava. There are cats. There are snails. I think anything could happen."

—Theo Von

"Life should not be a journey to the grave with the intention of arriving safely in a pretty and well-preserved body, but rather to skid in broadside in a cloud of smoke, thoroughly used up, totally worn out, and loudly proclaiming 'Wow, what a Ride!'"

—Hunter S. Thompson

PROLOGUE

"You have power over your mind—not outside events.
Realize this, and you will find strength."

—Marcus Aurelius

Whatever *your* goal in reading this book, you will not accomplish it unless you truly believe you have control to make decisions that affect your life.

Whether you are sitting at a computer, working on an assembly line, or getting ready to go to college, only one person is standing in your way of success and freedom: you.

There is never any person to blame.

There is never any situation to blame.

As difficult as it is, you must believe you are where you are because of the decisions you have made. You will get to where you are going based upon the decisions you will make.

If we blame someone or something for our lot in life, then we make it true. If we do that, we lose our agency. If we lose our agency, we lose our souls.

What you are about to undertake is hard. This is good news. If it were easy, everyone would do it. And it's the journey you'll remember in the end.

"Whatever the mind can conceive and believe, it can achieve."

—Napoleon Hill

PART 1

WHY THE OLD PLAYBOOK FAILED YOU

CHAPTER 1

THE DREAM WAS A LIE

(This is someone else's dream. It is not yours to have.)

WHAT NAPOLEON HILL SAID/WHAT IT MEANS NOW

WHAT HILL SAID (1937):

"Every person who wins in any undertaking must be willing to burn his ships and cut all sources of retreat."

WHAT IT MEANS NOW:

Today burning the ships means burning the *old expectations* that don't fit anymore. Success doesn't come from sticking closer to the herd. It comes from finding your own lane and owning it.

Everyone wants success.

But most people have been handed a broken map of how to get there.

You know the one:

- Go to school.

- Get good grades.

- Find a stable job.

- Climb the ladder.

- Retire happy at 65.

That map *might* have made sense in 1960. Perhaps 1980. But not today.

The truth is, **the dream is broken. It's been broken for a long time**. We've all known this, but most have done nothing to remedy it.

If *you* follow the traditional script without questioning it, you'll spend your best years running a race that doesn't lead where you think it does.

WHY THE OLD DREAM IS OVER

Let's look at the facts:

- **Student debt**. The average college graduate today leaves school with over **$37,000** in debt, and many never earn enough to pay it back comfortably (Federal Reserve, 2023).

- **Income stagnation**. After adjusting for inflation, **median real wages** in the United States have barely moved in **40 years** (Economic Policy Institute, 2019).

- **Retirement security**. Nearly **50 percent** of Americans approaching retirement have saved **less than $100,000** total (Northwestern Mutual, 2023).

- **20 years in retirement?** If a person lives to 65, the average life expectancy is another 20 years. With pensions gone and social security at risk, this group of people won't be able to afford basic living expenses (TIAA, 2024).

- **Homelessness**. The number of people who experience homelessness in the United States is **accelerating**, with 12 percent growth in 2023 and 18 percent growth in 2024. Today almost 1 million people try to survive each night without a house (National Alliance to End Homelessness).

- **Job satisfaction**. Gallup's global workplace report shows that only **23 percent** of workers feel "engaged" at work, meaning three out of four are just going through the motions. (Gallup)

- **Mental health crisis**. Rates of depression and anxiety among working adults have risen **by over 25** percent in the last decade alone (WHO, 2022). Two out of three young adults have experienced some kind of mental health issue in the past two years (The Annie E. Casey Foundation, 2024).

And the kicker:

- **We are in a crisis**. More young people can't afford a home (The Title Report). They are having less or no sex (*Time*). They are increasingly spending their time alone (American Psychiatric Association). And suicides of young Americans are up 56 percent in just a decade (American Academy of Pediatrics).

Here's the harsh truth: Most people following the "good job, good life" blueprint are **broke, stressed, unfulfilled, and trapped**.

The old dream isn't dead because people stopped working hard. It's dead because the game changed and nobody updated the playbook.

The question that kept haunting me before writing this book was, "If the system was designed to help us thrive, why are so many people drowning?"

I see it more and more every day.

Young people are struggling to find work. College left them with thousands of unpaid bills and didn't guarantee them an adequate-paying job or any means of support.

More of my friends are unemployed, underemployed, or extremely unhappy with their career path. In just the last month before finishing this book, three friends who have been with their companies for 10, 18, and 26 years, respectively, have all been laid off.

Those in our family who have retired are worried they don't have enough funds to support themselves, and quite a few who bought into the "retirement is bliss" fantasy have lost any and all purpose in their lives.

We must face the facts. The system wasn't built for us to thrive. It was built for a very small percentage of people to thrive.

We were promised a roadmap. Instead, we got a treadmill.

- Student debt is now a life sentence.

- Wages are flat but costs have exploded.

- The job ladder was sawed off.

- Burnout is now the norm.

- Retirement was never a real thing.

So what do you do when the path doesn't work? You build your own. And that starts with your Tilt.

TILT: THE NEW STARTING LINE

If you want to build something real today, you can't rely on institutions to hand you opportunities. Sure, working for someone else provides learning about processes you can't find online. It enables you to meet friends and colleagues that can assist you on your journey. But for the most part, you are trading in your valuable time so others can become rich and successful. (*Note: This is not necessarily bad, but you need to be aware of it.*)

You have to **create your own opportunities** by finding your **Tilt: your unique angle, expertise, obsession, and flavor that separates you from everyone else.**

As Warren Buffett and Simon Sinek discuss, every successful person is really good at one thing. That's your Tilt.

A Tilt isn't about being louder or flashier. It's about being **more specific, more real**, and **more essential** to a group of people who need exactly what you have.

And once you understand your Tilt and expose it to the world, you can build a freedom system around that one thing.

CASE STUDY: STEELY DAN—THE BAND THAT TILTED THE INDUSTRY

When Walter Becker and Donald Fagen started Steely Dan in the early 1970s, the music industry had a simple model:

- Tour relentlessly.
- Chase radio hits.
- Fit into a popular sound.

They refused.

Instead, they focused on **studio perfectionism**, recording obsessively until each track was exactly what they wanted. They blended **jazz, rock, and brainy** lyrics in a way nobody else did.

They rarely toured. They didn't chase Top 40 radio. They made records their way . . . slowly, carefully, brilliantly.

At first, they confused a lot of people. But by sticking to their Tilt, they built a loyal following that respected their precision, depth, and creativity.

Steely Dan became one of the most influential music acts of the 20th century. Not because they were "popular" in the traditional sense, but because they **owned a category no one else touched**.

Their Tilt *became their brand.*

You don't have to appeal to everyone. As Jay Acunzo often says, you only have to be someone's favorite. You have to matter deeply to someone (not everyone).

HOW TO FIND YOUR TILT

It wasn't long ago that humans were rewarded for fitting in and going along with the pack. That, thankfully, is no longer the case.

Now and into the future, freedom means leaning into what makes you different . . . your Tilt.

You don't need a master plan. You need a direction strong enough to start. So . . .

1. **List 10 things you're endlessly curious about**. There are no wrong answers here.

2. **Find the uncommon link**. Where are two or three ideas connecting in a way nobody's noticed?

3. **Pick an audience**. Who needs this? Who's underserved?

4. **Own the weirdness**. If you sound like everyone else, you're doing it wrong.

Adam Alter, a two-time *New York Times* bestselling author, discusses the concept of recombination. The idea is that finding originality today is nearly impossible. In his research with musicians and other artists, Alter states that all the building blocks around creating art have already been developed. So today we must recombine already developed elements into something that seems original.

When rock music was first created, was it new? You could argue that it wasn't.

In the late 1940s, country music and blues were extremely popular. Well, just add electric guitars and a steady drumbeat, and presto, rock 'n' roll!

This is exactly what a Tilt looks like. Your Tilt will be a recombination of elements from a variety of places that is something completely different.

And it's not rocket science, either.

Here are a few short, punchy examples of recombination topics that show how originality often comes from blending:

- **Tiny MBA**. Business lessons + daily comic strip format
- **FarmTok**. Traditional farming tips + TikTok trends
- **Mindful Strength**. Weightlifting + meditation
- **Parenting for Gamers**. Digital parenting + gamer culture
- **Crypto + History**. Blockchain concepts explained through ancient civilizations
- **Minimalist Travel**. Budget travel + extreme minimalism

Each takes familiar ingredients, mixes them in a new way, and creates a Tilt that feels fresh.

When I started in publishing, I was curious about marketing. With the rise of Google and, shortly after that, social media, I asked the question, "With all these places where consumers can find information, won't brands need to become excellent at publishing their own information and not always advertising?"

That practice, called "content marketing," became the driving marketing strategy of the 2010s. And it became my Tilt and, ultimately, my freedom.

Here are some Tilt examples:

- **Ann Handley**

  Writing that makes you a better marketer

  (*Tilt*: Clear, human, useful content . . . especially through newsletters and storytelling)

- **Jay Baer**

  Speed and trust as modern marketing strategy

  (*Tilt*: Evolved from word-of-mouth marketing to helping businesses get faster and more responsive in a noisy world)

- **Marcus Sheridan**

  Radical honesty through content that answers customer questions

  (*Tilt*: "They Ask, You Answer" sales-focused content built on transparency and education)

Non-marketing creator Tilts include:

- **Ali Abdaal**

  Productivity and study techniques for ambitious professionals

  (*Tilt*: Making self-improvement nerdy, efficient, and fun)

- **Cait Flanders**

  Mindful minimalism for conscious consumers

  (*Tilt*: Living with less, spending with intention, and writing deeply about it)

- **James Clear**

  Habit science simplified for everyday success

  (*Tilt*: Turning behavioral psychology into clear, practical daily actions)

- **MrBeast (Jimmy Donaldson)**

  Over-the-top generosity as entertainment

  (*Tilt*: Viral videos that push human extremes and reward others at scale)

- **Brené Brown**

  Emotional vulnerability as a leadership tool

  (*Tilt*: Bringing academic research into the heart of everyday relationships and culture)

- **Dude Perfect**

  Family-friendly trick shots as competitive spectacle

  (*Tilt*: Sports entertainment without profanity or controversy)

- **Not Boring (Packy McCormick)**

  Tech investing with storytelling flair

  (*Tilt*: Making complex business and venture topics feel exciting and optimistic)

- **Van Neistat (The Spirited Man)**

  Manual craftsmanship meets poetic life lessons

  (*Tilt*: Philosophical DIY filmmaking with a throwback aesthetic)

- **Emily Oster**

  Data-driven parenting advice

  (*Tilt*: Bringing economic analysis to family decision making: no judgment, just facts)

YOUR TILT WILL EVOLVE

You don't need to "get it right" forever. You just need to get specific enough to start.

You can refine your Tilt later. You can grow into it. You can pivot when the time comes.

But you can't build freedom from a place of generality.

Plus, being general is boring.

SANS TILT?

If you don't have a clue about what your Tilt is yet, don't stress. Investor Mark Cuban gives great advice about this: If you don't know what your differentiation is, expose yourself to as many new things as possible. Talk to people from different backgrounds. Go to a flea market. Check out a church. Go to a ball game. Read a book.

Visualize the movie *Batman Begins* (2005) when Bruce Wayne digs his way into what would become the bat cave. At this point, he's not Batman yet. He stumbles upon an area infested with bats. At first, he ducks. The bats are darting every which way. Then he stands up and accepts the bats as they circle around him. It's at that point Bruce Wayne becomes Batman—his true purpose (*a bit corny, but true*).

Before you find your Tilt, activities will dart around you like they have no specific purpose. But if you lean into all these different activities, they'll start to make sense to you, and you'll begin to realize your true purpose. Once you accept this, you'll be more open to who you can and will become.

Important note: If you need to know more about an area to find your Tilt . . . your true purpose . . . go do the thing. Take the crappy job and learn the skills. Do the internship. Talk to the person who has done the job. Ask to follow someone for a week and write down everything that person does.

After graduating with a master's degree from Penn State University, I had the large challenge of finding a job. Or rather, I couldn't find anything. Simply put, I was overeducated and underexperienced (a horrible and deadly combination).

I sent out hundreds of letters to employers with no luck. At my lowest, one of my friends recommended a temp agency. So . . .I started doing temp work inside banks and insurance companies for a week at a time. For three months I did temp jobs all over the Cleveland, Ohio, area.

And then, out of nowhere, I was offered full-time internal communications work at an insurance company. For three years I learned the Microsoft system inside and out and learned to deal with all sorts of amazing and difficult people.

And then, because I knew Microsoft Access and could project-manage, I received a job interview at Penton Media. My time at Penton eventually led me to the idea of content marketing. The rest is history.

APPLE AND VISION

In 1997, Apple, the company, was floundering. With it losing billions and lacking any clear direction, its once high-flying stock sank (on a split-adjusted basis) below a dollar per share. Every analyst left Apple for dead.

In July of that year, Apple fired its CEO and named **Steve Jobs** (recently back with the company after Apple acquired NeXT) interim CEO. By September, the company's stock dropped even further.

You know how the story turns out. The iPod, iTunes, the iPhone, the iPad, AirPods . . . all amazing successes. Apple became the first company ever to reach a trillion-dollar valuation. If you purchased Apple stock in 1997 and held it, you would have seen gains of 25,000+ percent. A $10,000 investment would be worth millions.

But it wasn't the products that started this turnaround. It was Apple's Tilt.

On September 23, 1997, Apple held an internal meeting about the launch of the company's new focus, called "Think Different." In the first five minutes, Steve Jobs talked about where Apple was going wrong. In short, Apple had started communicating to customers about how good its computers were. All their features and benefits. Jobs believed Apple lost its way with that kind of communication.

Then he talked about Apple's purpose. Its reason for being. He said, " . . . we need to get back to our core value . . . that people with passion change the world for the better." Jobs said that while Apple's products were certainly important, it was way more important to focus on what made Apple different from IBM and HP and every other computer company. From that moment, Apple stopped talking about the product's features and benefits and started talking about what Apple stood for. In other words, the Tilt.

The results speak for themselves. From that moment on, because of this renewed focus on purpose, Apple changed everything about the company. With it, the product roadmap changed, and now you are probably holding an iPhone because of it.

LET'S GO!

The old dream was mass market, mass career, mass identity.

The new world demands precision, passion, and purpose.

Find your Tilt. Own it. Grow it.

Don't chase someone else's ladder. **Build your own world**.

That's how you start burning the playbook.

"Be so good they can't ignore you."

—Steve Martin

PART II:

THE RECIPE FOR A NEW WORLD

CHAPTER 2

BELIEF OVER PROOF

(Belief before results. Trust the process.)

WHAT HILL SAID/WHAT IT MEANS NOW

WHAT HILL SAID (1937):

"Faith is the 'eternal elixir' which gives life, power, and action to the impulse of thought."

WHAT IT MEANS NOW:

Belief isn't some mystical force. It's practical survival. It's what separates the ones who last from the ones who almost made it.

Never say you can't do it. Say you haven't done it yet.

—*Rick Rubin*

If you're waiting for someone to tell you you're good enough, ready enough, or credible enough, you'll be waiting your whole life.

Belief has to come first. Before the audience. Before the proof. Before the numbers make sense.

If you want to build something that matters, you must **believe without evidence** . . . long enough for the evidence to catch up.

WHY YOU MUST BELIEVE FIRST

The world doesn't hand out early validation. Here's why:

- **Creator traction timeline.** It takes the average full-time creator **18 to 24 months** of consistent publishing before reaching sustainable revenue (Tilt Creator Economy Benchmark study, 2023). Some of the greatest creator examples I know didn't reach profitability for three years or more. It took four years for our company to reach profitability.

- **Trust curve.** Research shows it takes **50–70+ touchpoints** (posts, videos, interactions) before someone fully trusts a new brand or creator (Edelman Trust Barometer, 2022).

- **Business survival rates.** Over **65 percent** of new businesses don't make it past year five; not because they weren't necessarily good, but because they didn't survive long enough to break through (U.S. Small Business Administration Statistics, 2023).

You won't get proof early because **trust is slow** and **momentum is invisible at first**.

Virality that builds an audience happens after putting out valuable information, in some cases, thousands of times.

If you quit because no one noticed you yet, you're quitting five minutes before the compound effect kicks in.

I ALMOST GAVE UP

My company was losing money two years into my content marketing blog. In September 2009 I lost my biggest-paying client and was ready to pack it in.

After two weeks (and updating my LinkedIn profile in case I needed to find a job), I decided to redouble my efforts. Why? I didn't want to work for someone else . . . ever again.

I went back to the drawing board, changing the name of the company to Content Marketing Institute, with plans to launch a magazine and an international event.

We relaunched in May 2010.

Less than two years later we were a multimillion-dollar company.

Three years after that we sold the company for approximately $30 million.

The point? Building an audience takes time. Finding the right Tilt and approach takes time. Understanding what people will buy from you takes time.

Believe in yourself and trust the process.

THE ART OF NOT LISTENING

Gary Vaynerchuck says that **not listening to what others think** is the single most important thing you can do to succeed in life. If you can do that, you will listen to no one but yourself.

"First and foremost, be kind and empathetic and loving with yourself."

—Gary Vaynerchuck

When I announced that I was going to launch Content Marketing World, what became the largest event in the industry, my friends scoffed and joked. "Where will you be hosting the 27 people?" is an exact quote.

Tune out the noise. Almost everyone will think you are crazy. Let them. Focus on the people who support you and ignore the rest.

Entrepreneur Alex Hormozi says the same: "Once you've already won, people are like 'He's amazing' or 'She's so good.' That's the time when you need it the least. You always have to be the one that roots for you before anyone else does."

CASE STUDY: MARQUES BROWNLEE'S INVISIBLE YEARS

Today Marques Brownlee (MKBHD) is one of the biggest tech voices on YouTube, with tens of millions of subscribers.

But rewind to 2008:

- He was a teenager uploading blurry tech reviews from his bedroom.
- He had no brand deals.
- He had no viral moments.
- He had no money.

For *five years* he posted into the void. Slow, patient, deliberate. Video after video after video. With no guarantee anyone would ever care.

He didn't "go viral." He outlasted everyone else.

Marques didn't wait for proof. He kept moving until proof arrived.

THE SCIENCE BEHIND BELIEF

In psychology, there's a concept called "self-efficacy." **Self-efficacy** is the belief in your ability to succeed at specific tasks. Study after study shows that **belief often precedes actual success**.

When you believe you can improve, you persist longer. When you persist longer, you get better. When you get better, results start to appear.

No belief = no effort = no improvement = no success

Belief isn't a luxury. It's a **strategy.**

BELIEVE IT AND MAKE IT REAL

Neuroscientist Dr. Tara Swart emphasizes that our brains are wired to reinforce the narratives we tell ourselves. When we consistently affirm a belief, whether positive or negative, our brain's **neuroplasticity** enables the formation of neural pathways that support this belief. This means that by consciously choosing empowering thoughts, we can rewire our brains to foster confidence and resilience, effectively shaping our reality through intentional belief.

My friend Scott Monty often cites the work of William James, the father of modern sports psychology. James discovered what he called "**precursive faith.**" Basically, **precursive faith** is the belief that you can do something, even if you've never tried it before.

In essence: If you believe you can, your brain rewires itself for that belief. If you believe you can't, your brain also makes sure that is the case. So . . . **whatever you believe, that is the answer.**

HOW BARBARA CORCORAN REWIRED HER WAY TO MILLIONS

Before she became a *Shark Tank* legend, Barbara Corcoran had **zero business experience**, 23 different jobs, and a self-described "C student" mentality. But what made her dangerous? She trained herself to see rejection as fuel.

Barbara's early real estate career was full of setbacks. Her boyfriend and business partner dumped her and told her she'd never succeed without him.

Instead of collapsing, she consciously rewired her narrative.

Every time she was told no, she tracked it. She treated rejection like data, not failure. She reframed each "no" into proof that she was on the right path. An act of deliberate mental rewiring.

She built small wins into neural momentum. Each closed deal trained her brain to trust herself. Eventually, she grew The Corcoran Group into one of New York's top real estate firms, selling it for $66 million.

THE INVISIBLE YEARS ARE NORMAL

What nobody tells you when you start:

- Your first dozen posts will feel invisible.

- Your first 50 podcast episodes will sound amateurish.

- Your first two years of building might look like "failure" from the outside.

Good. It means you're doing it right. Everyone looks like they're losing at the beginning.

SEAN CONNERY AND HAPPINESS

While reading the book *Travels* by Michael Crichton, I learned a bit about actor Sean Connery.

Apparently, Connery was an unhappy man when he first started out in acting. Small things would bother him. They would fester. He was mad all the time.

He decided to make a change. He said (this is a paraphrase), "As long as I'm here and alive today, I might as well be happy instead of miserable." From that day forward, he woke up each morning and made a choice to be happy. According to Crichton, Connery was one of the nicest and most interesting men he's ever met.

Connery made the decision and believed he could change. That's all it took. His brain handled the rest.

HOW TO BUILD BELIEF LIKE A CREATOR

You don't need a vision board. You need a rhythm.

Belief isn't something you force. It's something you build by showing up consistently when no one else is paying attention.

Here's how to do that:

1. **The rule of recurrence.** Repetition beats intensity. One post a week for a year is better than a 30-day sprint. The brain, and your audience, responds to patterns, not bursts.

2. **Build, publish, reflect.** Every piece of content is a brick in the house. Don't overthink each one. Publish it. Move on. But reflect weekly: What worked? What felt right? What didn't?

3. **Document over hype.** Don't try to impress. Just tell the truth. Share what you're learning, what you're building, and how you're thinking. Trust builds through honesty, not polish.

4. **Momentum is the goal.** You're not trying to go viral. You're trying to gain traction. Belief grows when you realize that momentum is self-made and fully within your control.

Researchers at University College London found that, on average, it takes **66 days** for a new behavior to become automatic. That means the early days of showing up, when it feels awkward, pointless, or invisible, aren't failures. They're the *necessary rewiring period*. If you commit to a task daily for two months, you're not just doing the thing . . . you're teaching your brain that *this is who you are now*. That's how belief becomes habit and then habit becomes identity.

THE BAMBOO GROWTH CURVE

Bamboo farmers plant seeds and water them daily. For the first **four years,** nothing appears above ground. But underground, a massive root system is forming. In year five, bamboo can grow **up to 90 feet in just five weeks**.

Building your Tilt, your audience, your independence? It's bamboo work. No visible growth for years. Massive acceleration afterward if you stay the course.

YOU HAVE NO COMPETITION

If goal setting were a skill, most Americans would be failing . . .significantly.

Let's look at the math.

In order to accomplish something, it makes sense to set a goal. Gallup says that, in general, 70 percent of U.S. adults set goals.

But according to a study by Dr. Michelle Rozen, just six percent of individuals who set goals at the beginning of the year are still pursuing them six months later. In a similar study, the University of Scranton found that over 90 percent of New Year's goals are never reached.

There are approximately 265 million adults in the United States. If 7 out of 10 set goals, that gets us to 186 million. Of those 186 million setting goals, those continuing to work on those goals just a few months later leave us with 10 million.

Stated differently, about four percent of the U.S. adult population sets and follows through with those goals after 12 months. The percentage of those who set and follow through with goals year after year is minuscule.

The hard truth is that we live in a society that gives up a lot, and at that right quickly.

If this is your competition, it's simply not a fair fight.

Consider two people: Alex and Jordan.

Both started the year with the same goal: to get in shape and run a half marathon. Alex did what most people do: bought new shoes, joined a gym, and posted about it on Instagram. Jordan also joined a gym, but did something different: Jordan set a 5 a.m. alarm every weekday and committed to showing up at the gym, no matter what.

Six months later, Alex is back on the couch, the gym membership untouched and the shoes collecting dust. Jordan? Ran their first race, didn't break any records, but finished and is now training for a full marathon.

The difference wasn't desire. It was consistency.

And here's the kicker: Jordan isn't superhuman. They just decided not to quit when it got boring, inconvenient, or hard. In a world where most people give up, simply staying in the game gives you an almost unfair advantage.

I say to my kids: **you really can accomplish anything you want in life**. They look at me and roll their eyes, like children will do with their parents.

But it's true. And if you can set and keep goals, you have an incredible advantage over anyone else out there because most people out there in your sphere—well, they give up.

The only one stopping you is you. End of story.

CHALAMET AND HATERS

In 2025, Timothée Chalamet won the Screen Actors Guild (SAG) Award for best actor for his portrayal of musician Bob Dylan. Upon acceptance, Chalamet had this to say:

"I know the classiest thing would be to downplay the effort that went into this role and how much this means to me, but the truth is this was five years of my life. I poured everything I had into playing this incomparable artist, Mr. Bob Dylan, a true American hero.

. . . I can't downplay the significance of this award. Cause it means the most to me. And I know we're in a subjective business, but the truth is, I'm really in pursuit of greatness. I know people don't usually talk like that, but I want to

be one of the greats. I'm inspired by the greats. I'm inspired by the greats here
tonight. I'm as inspired by Daniel Day-Lewis, Marlon Brando, and Viola
Davis as I am by Michael Jordan, Michael Phelps, and I want to be up there.
So I'm deeply grateful. This doesn't signify that, but it's a little more fuel. It's
a little more ammo to keep going. Thank you so much."

Many critics came out and said Chalamet was too egotistical. Too into himself. That he needed to tone things down.

But do they know what Chalamet did to train for the role?

- He learned to play guitar.
- He became a Bob Dylan historian, reading up on the musician to understand his childhood, his unique circumstances, and how he immersed himself into New York culture.
- He learned about 40 Dylan songs by heart.
- He worked with a dialect coach to approximate Dylan's nasal voice.
- He worked with a singing coach.
- He gained 20 pounds.

Chalamet had a vision. He did the work. He accomplished the goal.

Thankfully he doesn't listen to the media naysayers.

LET'S GO!

Proof doesn't come first. Belief does.

You won't always feel certain. You won't always feel seen. You won't always feel rewarded.

But the people who win are the ones who show up anyway.

Plant the seeds. Water the roots. Trust the invisible years.

Burn the playbook that says you need fast validation. Believe before the world tells you you're right.

CHAPTER 3

YOU ARE WHAT YOU REPEAT

(Daily reps beat motivation every time.)

WHAT HILL SAID/WHAT IT MEANS NOW

WHAT HILL SAID (1937):

"Any idea, plan, or purpose may be placed in the mind through repetition of thought."

WHAT IT MEANS NOW:

In today's world, repetition does more than plant an idea in your brain. It trains your audience to know, like, and trust you.

Motivation is unreliable. It fades after a good podcast. It disappears the second life gets hard. And if you're depending on it to carry your goals, you're already behind.

If belief is the fuel, then **repetition is the engine**. The creators who win don't work harder. They don't hustle louder. They **show up more consistently**, especially when no one's watching.

That's the edge. That's the game.

Effort is worth twice as much as talent.

—*Angela Duckworth, author of* Grit.

WHAT THE DATA SAYS ABOUT REPETITION AND RESULTS

According to a Duke University study, **over 40 percent of our daily behaviors are habits,** not conscious decisions. *Meaning*: You are, literally, what you repeat.

From the creator side: Only **six percent of full-time creators** hit meaningful financial traction in their first year. But that number triples for those who persist into their third year (Tilt Creator Economy Benchmark study, 2023).

Even in music: ScienceDirect found that **greater repetition in a song,** in both the chorus and the words, significantly increases the likelihood the song will be popular with more people.

The results come to the ones (and words) who last.

CASE STUDY: JAMES CLEAR AND THE ATOMIC REPETITION LOOP

Before *Atomic Habits*, James Clear was a consistent but unknown blogger.

He published every Monday and Thursday for years. No ads. No hype. Just consistency.

That rhythm built trust with readers. It sharpened his ideas. And when the time came to publish his book, he had the audience, credibility, and reps to make it a hit.

With over 10 million copies sold, the lesson is clear: **The most powerful habits start when no one's watching**.

THE 1,000-REPS RULE

In baseball, there's a coaching principle that says a hitter needs **1,000 repetitions** of a new motion before it becomes second nature.

- If you want to change your swing? 1,000 reps.
- If you want to improve your fielding? 1,000 reps.

That's not because players are unmotivated. It's because muscle memory doesn't care about motivation. It cares about **repetition**.

The same is true for creators. Your voice, your style, your authority? It comes from the reps.

THE THREE RE'S: A SIMPLE SYSTEM THAT BUILDS MOMENTUM

You don't need another app. You need a pen, a notebook, and this:

1. RECORD

Write your goal in the present tense:

- "I finished my novel."
- "I'm building a six-figure coaching business."
- "I publish weekly to 10,000 subscribers."

If you don't write it, you don't own it.

2. REPEAT

Read it every morning and every night.

Repetition builds identity. Your brain doesn't know the difference between imagination and memory. It will start believing what it sees every day.

3. REMOVE

Eliminate distractions that sabotage progress.

Distractions cost creators **up to 40 percent of productive time** daily, according to a UC Irvine study. Remove clutter, notifications, and wasted energy. Check your phone time.

Protect your bandwidth like your income depends on it. Because it does.

"If you do not know what you want . . . if you can't write it down . . . you can't have it."

—Bruce Lipton

S.M.A.R.T. GOALS

When I first started out, my mentor Jim McDermott turned me on to Brian Tracy's goal-setting system—S.M.A.R.T.:

Specific. Instead of "grow sales," we want to include how much revenue and in what kind of time frame.

Measurable. Goals must be quantified. If they aren't, we can't measure them.

Achievable. Goals must be challenging but realistic.

Relevant. Goals should align with our life, career mission, and Tilt.

Time-bound. We need to set a date to accomplish the goal and then work the plan backward from that date.

This process led directly to the goal of, ultimately, selling my business.

In January of 2008 I wrote, "My wife and I sell the company in 2015 for $15 million." This is the goal that I reviewed every morning and that paved the way for our ultimate exit in June 2016.

S.M.A.R.T.!

BEHAVIOR FOLLOWS IDENTITY

When you repeat a habit long enough, it becomes part of who you are.

- You're not trying to *write a book*.

  You're becoming someone who writes.

- You're not trying to *start a podcast*.

  You're becoming someone who publishes with clarity and consistency.

- Your goal isn't to *finish something flashy*.

  Your goal is to **become someone who follows through**.

I had a conversation with my youngest about going to college. The premise? Since we can learn everything online today, what's the purpose of college? Why do so many employers still require a college education for a particular job?

My take: Maybe getting a degree is not about the education per se. A degree means to you that you finished something. You went to class consistently. You showed up. You did the work. You took on a project and saw it through to the end. You followed through.

Honestly, who cares what anyone thinks, college degree or not? You finishing something big like that tells your brain that you are a finisher. You did the work over and over and over again and finished. That's important.

THE TRUST BUCKET

Each time you publish, you add a drop into the trust bucket; yours and your audience's.

At first, it looks like nothing is happening. Then, slowly, it fills. And then all at once, the trust overflows.

People will call it a breakthrough. But you'll know it was just **Tuesday**. The 42nd article or podcast or video in a row.

"NORM!" AND THE TWO PARTS TO CONSISTENCY

Growing up, I watched the NBC hit show *Cheers* every Thursday. One of the main characters was Norm Peterson. Everybody loved Norm. So much so that when he entered the Cheers bar, all the other patrons yelled out "Norm!"

Why did everyone love Norm?

Well, first, because he showed up at the same time every day. **To be loved, you must be present**.

Second, Norm always had **something interesting** to say. Every. Single. Time.

It went like this:

Norm: *"Afternoon, everybody."*

Everyone in the bar: *"Norm!"*

Bartender or patron: *"How's the world been treating you?"*

Norm: *"Like a baby treats a diaper."*

To be great, you must be consistent in two ways. First, you must show up. Second, you must be interesting. Every. Single. Time.

Anthony Fasano, a content entrepreneur who built the Engineering Management Institute, says it this way:

"Consistency in content publication is critical. First, consistency, in life, is critical. If you go to the gym once a month, it doesn't help you. If you go multiple times a week, it helps you. If you eat good once a month, it doesn't help you. The same thing goes with content. If you do a podcast every so often, whenever you get the creative itch, you're not really helping anyone because it's just too random. There's no strategy around it.

You must force yourself to do it because otherwise you're not going to get into a rhythm. Your audience is not going to be feeling that they're getting the value on a consistent basis, and you won't build channels where you can impact and influence a lot of people and help a lot of people, quite frankly."

Perfectly said.

LET'S GO!

The world doesn't reward your intentions. It rewards your rhythm.

Want better results? Build better repetitions.

Write. Post. Build. Rest. Reflect. Repeat.

Burn the playbook that says motivation creates momentum. Repetition is how freedom is built. Brick by brick, rep by rep.

CHAPTER 4

EXPERTISE BEATS CREDENTIALS

(Learn what matters. Ignore what doesn't.)

WHAT HILL SAID/WHAT IT MEANS NOW

WHAT HILL SAID (1937):

> *"Successful people, in all callings, never stop acquiring specialized knowledge."*

WHAT IT MEANS NOW:

Today specialized knowledge doesn't just make you valuable. It makes you discoverable. Depth is the shortcut to trust.

Most of what we were taught about authority is wrong.

You were probably told:

- Get good grades.

- Earn a degree.

- Accumulate titles.

- Let someone else decide when you're qualified.

But today? That model is shattered.

We're in a world where credibility doesn't come from letters after your name. It comes from how clearly and consistently you solve real problems.

THE COLLAPSE OF THE GATEKEEPERS

A decade ago, if you wanted to teach or advise others, you needed to go through a system:

- Academia

- Corporate ladders

- Publishing houses

- Conference committees

Not anymore.

Now your audience is the gatekeeper. And their question isn't "Where did you study?"

It's "Can you help me with this problem right now?"

A few months before finishing this book, I took a call with a recent college graduate. They asked all sorts of questions, but the big one revolved around "How do I find a job in this market?"

They wanted to find a role in marketing at a Cleveland-area enterprise.

"Okay," I said. "If that's what you want, build an audience."

After a few seconds of no response, I expanded:

"Marketing today is about creating a true differentiation, understanding how to tell a story over a long period of time, and building an audience that knows, likes, and trusts you so they will ultimately buy from you.

Well, you can do that now. *Take any one of your interests or curiosities. Create a newsletter. Build a YouTube channel. Start a podcast. It could be about catching butterflies to release in manufacturing plants to create better airflow. The more specific, the better (remember your Tilt).*

Once you build an audience, you'll be qualified for just about any marketing position. You don't have to wait for the right credentials or experiences. Just do it yourself."

And the good news? Once you build an audience, not only are you creating better options for getting a job . . . **you are building the foundations of a business that will set you free**.

WHAT THE DATA SAYS

According to LinkedIn's "Future of Work" report, **skills-based hiring** has increased **by 21 percent** in the last two years while degree requirements have steadily dropped across most job sectors.

YouTube is the **second-largest search engine in the world**. Millions of people are learning from creators, not institutions.

Platforms like Substack and Patreon are growing because people are willing to **pay directly** for niche expertise they can apply now.

Expertise is no longer bestowed. It's built.

CASE STUDY: EMILY OSTER—AN ECONOMIST IN THE PARENTING WORLD

Emily Oster isn't a pediatrician. She's an economist.

Yet she's become one of the most trusted voices in parenting, not because she followed the traditional path, but because she carved a new one. She applies economic analysis and real data to decisions parents struggle with: sleep training, daycare, breastfeeding, screen time.

Why do people trust her?

Because she delivers *clarity* when the experts deliver *confusion*. That's the new authority: **specificity, usefulness, and transparency.**

HOW TO BUILD EXPERTISE THAT MATTERS

You don't need to know everything. You need to go deep enough to be useful.

Here's the modern expert checklist:

1. **Start with obsessive curiosity.** If you can't shut up about it, it's probably a Tilt. Follow that.

2. **Share what you learn in real time.** Teach in public. Document the journey. People love learning from someone who's *one step ahead.*

3. **Build a vault of content.** If someone searches your topic and finds *you*, you've already won. Make your ideas searchable and solve a problem.

4. **Focus on transformation, not trivia.** Can your content change someone's day, decision, or direction? If yes, you're an expert. Even without a certificate.

YOU CAN NEVER GO TOO NICHE

One of the biggest creator fears is that a person's Tilt is *too specific*. That if they focus on something too narrow, no one will care.

But the truth is, **specificity is your superpower.** You literally cannot be too specific.

When you try to reach everyone, you end up reaching no one. But when you go ultra-niche, when you focus on one tight audience with one urgent problem, you become essential.

You stop being just "a voice." You become *the voice*.

There are entrepreneurs who:

- Teach spreadsheet formulas *just for real estate agents* (https://www.youtube.com/@BreakIntoCRE).
- Run newsletters on *Midwestern craft beer* (https://thefullpint.com/).
- Have a midlife growth site focused on the longevity economy (https://further.net/).

And they're crushing it. Why? Because they're not trying to be famous. They're trying to be **useful**.

The internet rewards **focus and clarity**. The riches, as they say, are in the niches.

If you ever feel like your topic is "too small," you're probably on the right path.

CREATE YOUR OWN CATEGORY

The easiest way to build a loyal audience is to become the leading informational expert in your industry niche.

It takes years, sometimes decades, to publish enough consistently amazing information to build a loyal and trusting audience.

How can you shorten the time in making this happen?

Create a category.

I started in the custom publishing industry in 2000 and began selling custom publishing services to marketers the next year. I found out, very quickly, that the term "custom publishing" didn't resonate with my prospects, who were senior-level marketers.

The truth is, when I would open my mouth and say "custom publishing", they would pretty much fall asleep. Why would marketers care about publishing?

And yet this was a really important area of marketing. I believed that all innovative companies would need to create consistent and valuable information for their customers as publishing channels like blogs and social media opened, and that search engines like Google would be incredibly important.

I believed the industry term was the problem.

I tested out terms like "custom content" and "branded content" and "custom media." Nope, nope, and nope. Then I realized that all major marketing categories have the word "marketing" in it (I know, not exactly rocket science). "Direct marketing." "Search engine marketing." "Email marketing." So, I thought, why not "content marketing"?

When I mentioned content marketing in sales pitches with marketers, it immediately resonated. Mind you, they didn't know what it was, but it had "marketing" in it, so it must be for them.

I tested the term for years and ultimately believed it would become the industry term in this fast-growing area of marketing.

After leaving my job, my first-ever post on April 26, 2007, was called "Why Content Marketing?" It's a horrible post, but it was me telling the world and the three readers of my blog that I was committing to the term.

In order to create a category, there must be little to no competition for that term in the marketplace. I went over to Google Trends to check. I found good news. The term was barely being used.

This meant that if I could create a solid content strategy and get people to start using the term, we could become *the* resource for those people when they were ready.

There were three steps to the process:

The base. We had to choose a place on the web where we could create valuable information over a long period of time to start building an audience. We chose a blog.

The tent-pole piece. We needed to create a huge piece of content that the industry could not ignore. We created the "Content Marketing State of the Industry Report." Original research is so underused and underrated. A few years later we developed *The Story of Content*, a content marketing documentary. It's been viewed over a million times.

Influencer support. We needed to find smart people with audiences to help carry the term forward. To do this, we created the *Top Content Marketing Blogs* (which didn't include our own blog) that highlighted websites we thought were content marketing–focused but maybe those influencers weren't using the term just yet.

We put our heads down and did the work and by the beginning of 2010, content marketing was starting to become the industry term. Anytime anyone searched for anything content marketing on the web, our information would show up. It was amazing.

Today, it *is* the industry term.

Developing an audience is challenging at best. Building a category makes that process easier.

THE STAIRWELL, NOT THE STAGE

You don't need to stand on a stage to be seen. You need to be a **few steps ahead** on the staircase and willing to reach back.

Most audiences don't want a genius. They want a guide. Someone who speaks their language, remembers what it's like to be unsure, and can show them what worked.

That's you. A guide is usually expert enough. If you're learning, sharing, and applying, it's already happening.

LET'S GO!

Stop waiting for a degree, a job title, or a viral post to validate you.

If you're solving a real problem for real people in a consistent way, **you're already an expert**.

Burn the playbook that says authority is granted. Today, it's earned . . . through depth, usefulness, and truth.

CHAPTER 5

CREATE LIKE AN ARTIST. SELL LIKE A PRO.

(You can be both a creator and an entrepreneur.)

WHAT HILL SAID/WHAT IT MEANS NOW

WHAT HILL SAID (1937):

"Ideas are the beginning points of all fortunes."

WHAT IT MEANS NOW:

Ideas are worthless unless they ship (as Seth Godin so famously said). Don't wait for the idea. Make the decision and go. If it's not exactly right, you now know one thing you didn't before.

Somewhere along the way, we were told a lie: "You can be creative, or you can make money. Not both."

It's the myth of the starving artist. And while in some cases this is true, it doesn't have to be. You can write, film, speak, paint, teach, or coach **and** get paid. You can lead with passion **and** make a profit. You can build something that's art **and** something that lasts.

This isn't a choice between purity and capitalism. It's about building a life that funds your creativity, not stifles it.

THE OLD DIVIDE: ARTIST VERSUS BUSINESS

Traditionally, artists were told to:

- "Make something beautiful."
- "Starve for a while."
- "Hope someone buys it eventually."

Entrepreneurs were told to:

- "Find a market gap."
- "Solve a problem."
- "Scale at all costs."

But in today's creator economy, those worlds have collapsed into one. The most successful creator businesses (content entrepreneurs) are both:

- They lead with generosity, curiosity, and originality.
- They follow up with clarity, structure, and a business model.

AMANDA PALMER AND THE ART OF ASKING

Amanda Palmer is a musician who walked away from a major label and built her own direct connection with fans.

She built a model based on **trust and value exchange**, not middlemen.

Her TED Talk, *"The Art of Asking,"* led to one of the largest crowdfunded music campaigns in history. Not because she played it safe. But because she led with *truth, then transaction.*

She didn't stop being an artist. She just got better at **being in business**.

WHAT MODERN CREATORS DO DIFFERENTLY

1. **They give first . . . but with structure.** Free content builds trust. Paid content builds freedom. You need both.

2. **They make offers unapologetically.** Selling is not an interruption. It's an invitation. If fans know, like, and trust you, they will be willing to support you.

3. **They turn creative output into assets.**

   - Podcast episode → membership
   - Newsletter post → book chapter
   - Livestream → paid workshop

Everything you make can have a second, third, and fourth life.

THE THREE-PART CREATIVE REVENUE MODEL

To keep things simple, here's a go-to structure I often recommend:

1. **Free, consistent content.** Weekly newsletter. Podcast. Blog. YouTube channel. This is your trust-building engine. Your base.

2. **Low-ticket, high-value product.** Book. Guide. Mini course. Something that delivers real value for under $100. This is your first step to conversion.

3. **Flagship offering.** Coaching. Membership. Deep-dive course. Speaking. This is where your creative engine starts generating real independence.

You don't need to start with all three. But you do need to *start*.

If you decide to start on a platform that doesn't have a direct connection with a subscriber (such as TikTok, YouTube, or Instagram), you'll ultimately need a plan to **move those fans over to something you can control** (like a newsletter or Substack). In some local cases, SMS is catching on. This is to protect you if the platform ever changes the rules (and they always do). Something to always keep in mind.

Simple rule . . . if you don't know their email address, physical address, or phone number, you don't have a direct connection.

SHIP YOUR ART

Seth Godin's *The Bootstrapper's Bible* was invaluable to me before I launched my first business. To this day I keep a copy near my desk.

He's also one of the most prolific creators of the modern era. But ask him what separates professionals from amateurs, and he won't say talent. Or strategy. Or even luck.

He'll say this: **They ship.**

Godin believes that too many creators get stuck perfecting, polishing, and preparing. They wait for the masterpiece. They tinker endlessly. And they never publish.

He calls this the "resistance." The voice in your head that says, "It's not ready." "You're not good enough." "People will judge you."

His solution? **Ship it anyway.**

Early in his career, Godin started writing a daily blog . . . short posts, sometimes a single idea. But he didn't miss a day. Didn't overthink it. Just showed up, wrote, and shipped. One post at a time, he built a tribe. A voice. A reputation for clarity.

"Real artists ship," he says. Not someday. Not when it's perfect. *Today.* Because the act of finishing and sharing is what transforms ideas into impact.

CREATORS WHO BLENDED ART AND BUSINESS WITHOUT SELLING OUT

- **Becky Blades**. Artist and entrepreneur who self-published *Do Your Laundry or You'll Die Alone*, now used in high schools and universities as a life guide.
- **Shayda Campbell**. Watercolor artist who built a YouTube audience, sells online courses, and licenses her designs, all from her home studio.
- **Sorelle Amore**. Photographer and YouTuber who turned travel content into a personal brand, book deal, investment portfolio, and online education business.
- **Mason Currey**. Author of *Daily Rituals*, a passion project about artists' routines. The book sold well, then led to speaking gigs and a thriving paid newsletter.
- **Jack Butcher**. Visual designer who built a business around "Visualize Value," selling clarity through simple graphics and powerful digital products.

Each of these creators:

- Started with a curiosity or creative itch
- Built a system around their work
- Monetized without compromising their message

You don't have to be famous. You don't have to be loud. You just have to be **clear, consistent, and creative**.

BUILD THE SHELF

Every time you create something (a book, a talk, a framework, a product), imagine you're placing it on a **shelf behind you**.

You may not sell it today. But one day someone will walk through your world and look at that shelf, and it'll be exactly what they need.

Artists make. Pros build shelves.

YOU'RE NOT SELLING. YOU'RE SOLVING

People don't pay for content. They pay for change.

They want to:

- Save time.
- Make money.
- Avoid stress.
- Find meaning.
- Get clarity.
- Stop pain.

If your product helps people with any of that, you have a moral obligation to offer it. Not just for your business, **but for their benefit**.

Think about solving the need first, in both your content and your product. If you can keep your eye on helping, you'll generally make the right decision.

LET'S GO!

Stop separating creativity from commerce. Stop apologizing for wanting to be paid for your ideas.

You don't need to wait for permission to build something beautiful **and** profitable.

Burn the playbook that says artists must starve. You can create like an artist and sell like a pro.

PART III:

BUILDING FREEDOM THAT LASTS

CHAPTER 6

FOCUS IS FREEDOM

(Clarity beats chaos. Decide and commit.)

WHAT HILL SAID/WHAT IT MEANS NOW

WHAT HILL SAID (1937):

> *"There is one quality which one must possess to win, and that is definiteness of purpose . . . the knowledge of what one wants, and a burning desire to possess it."*

WHAT IT MEANS NOW:

Pick your move. Define your lane. Say no to everything that doesn't push you toward it.

Most creators don't fail from a lack of ideas. They fail because they try to chase all of them at once.

If you're building a business, **focus is your advantage**. The more clearly you define your one big move, the faster you gain traction and the less energy you waste on distractions disguised as opportunities.

As a wise person once said, "You can have as many cats as you want, but to keep them alive you have to feed them all."

This chapter is about finding and committing to your big move.

THE ILLUSION OF "MORE"

More platforms. More tactics. More products. More noise.

Creators get stuck trying to be everywhere, do everything, and serve everyone. And what happens? Nothing moves. Nothing sticks.

More options = more dilution

Focus isn't just efficient. It's magnetic. When you go all in on one idea, one channel, one product, people can finally *see* you.

WHAT THE DATA SAYS

- Creators who focus on **one primary platform** grow 3x faster in audience and revenue than those who try to master 3+ at once (Kit, 2023).

- In the early stages of a business, "decision fatigue" is one of the top reasons entrepreneurs burn out. Simplifying your strategy preserves momentum and creative energy.

- Warren Buffett famously said, "The difference between successful people and really successful people is that really successful people say no to almost everything."

THE GOLDEN RULE

This is the filter I've used for years. Every time a new opportunity pops up (and it will), run it through this filter:

- Does it build your audience?

- Does it build your asset?

- Does it serve your long game?

If not, it's a no.

You don't need a to-do list. You need a **don't-do list**.

CASE STUDY: MARIE FORLEO—ALL IN ON THE FLAGSHIP

Marie Forleo built her business around one central product: **B-School**.

While others scattered across offers and launches, she committed to one big program and made it better every year.

She created:

- Evergreen content on YouTube

- A free weekly newsletter

- A launch strategy that drove urgency and community

- A waitlist that kept demand high

The result? One product. Multiple eight-figure years. And a brand synonymous with impact.

Marie didn't build ten things halfway. She built one thing all the way.

THE FOCUS FILTER

Say no faster. Build momentum sooner.

Use this quick filter to evaluate any new opportunity, idea, or distraction. If it doesn't pass at least three of these five, it's a *no* for now.

- **Does it align with my current Tilt?** If it doesn't deepen your niche, it distracts from it.

- **Does it directly build my audience or asset?** Audience = trust. Asset = leverage. Everything else is noise.

- **Can I do this consistently for 6-12 months?** If not, it's a hobby or a distraction, not a strategy.

- **Will this move me closer to my one big goal?** Clarity dies when you chase parallel priorities.

- **Would future me thank present me for doing this now?** If not, it might be ego or FOMO driving the decision.

Score

- 5/5 = go. Lock it in.

- 3-4 = maybe. Park it in your "Later" list.

- 0-2 = nope. Burn it.

Bonus tip: Revisit your active projects once per month using this filter. Most of your best breakthroughs come from cutting, not adding.

HOW TO PLUG THE ENERGY LEAKS

Here's how to get ruthless about where your attention goes:

1. **Pick one core platform.** Instagram, YouTube, podcast, email . . . pick one. Dominate it. Everything else is secondary.

2. **Pick one core product or offer.** What are you known for? Focus your effort there. You can always expand later.

3. **Schedule your deep work.** If it's not on your calendar, it doesn't exist. Protect 90–120 minutes a day for focused creation.

4. **Audit your input.** Turn off notifications. Unfollow noise. Unsubscribe ruthlessly.

5. **Track where your time is leaking.** Where does your energy go that doesn't return results? Eliminate or automate it.

GO BIG OR GO HOME

When my content marketing blog finally started to build an audience, we received enough feedback to believe there was an opportunity to create an event for marketers around the practice of content marketing.

The safe route would have been to create a small workshop to test the idea. Instead, we decided to make our big move and seek to create the largest content marketing event in the world (in Cleveland, Ohio, of all places).

We thought, if we do this right, this could happen in a few years.

Our big bet paid off and in the first year 660 people showed up, making it the largest physical content marketing event in the world in year one. Four years later, 4,000 people showed up.

As my wife says, "Go big or go home."

When you go deep into one area:

- You create signature intellectual property (IP).

- You build authority faster.

- You remove friction from your audience's decision making.

People want a trusted guide, not a generalist who "sort of" does everything.

YOU WILL FEEL UNCOMFORTABLE

As David Bowie notes:

"If you [the artist] feel safe in the area you are working in, you're not working in the right area. Always go a little further into the water than you feel you're

capable of being in. Go a little bit out of your depth. And when you don't feel that your feet are quite touching the bottom, you're just about in the right place to do something exciting."

Think about your own writing, videos, podcasts . . . whatever it might be. When I think back on when I started blogging on content marketing, I remember sweating and feeling a little sick inside right before I pushed the publish button on those early posts. In those days, I was really pushing the establishment custom publishing industry. I was telling people they were wrong. I was setting new terminology. I was totally audacious, *and it scared the crap out of me.*

But I believed I was right and that people needed to hear these things. What I was creating was different than everything out there. And it was not safe. And it worked. That blog today has over 250,000 email subscribers, and the business continues to flourish.

Be honest with yourself. Challenge yourself. You'll be uncomfortable with some of what you create . . . and that's okay.

NOTRE DAME MAKES A BIG MOVE

In 2019 I took a trip to the University of Notre Dame in South Bend, Indiana, with my two kids. While spending time with the brothers of the Congregation of Holy Cross, we learned about the founding of the university. On November 26, 1842, a French priest named Father Edward Sorin, along with seven brothers and priests, took possession of over 500 acres of Indiana land given to them by the bishop with one goal on mind . . . to build a college.

According to the archives, the weather at that time was horrific and included lower-than-average temperatures, howling winds, and deep, deep snow. Oh, and the land was miles from any sort of civilization (in the middle of nowhere would not be an exaggeration).

But the bishop at that time believed that a school in that area would do an immense amount of good and Fr. Sorin believed in the bishop's vision. In Fr. Sorin's letter to Father Basil Moreau (founder of the Congregation of Holy Cross), he expands on the bishop's vision:

"As there is no other school within more than a hundred miles, this college cannot fail to succeed. . . . Before long, it will develop on a large scale. . . . It will be one of the most powerful means for good in this country."

Fourteen months later, on January 15, 1844, the university was officially chartered by the Indiana legislature.

Make the decision. Set the vision. Create the momentum.

LET'S GO!

You don't need to do more. You need to go deeper on what's already working or what you believe in most.

Focus. Make the move. Commit to the lane. Say no to the rest.

Burn the playbook that says more is better. One big move beats a thousand little ones. Every time.

CHAPTER 7

BUILD ONCE. SELL FOREVER.

(Create assets that work while you sleep.)

WHAT HILL SAID/WHAT IT MEANS NOW

WHAT HILL SAID (1937):

"Opportunity often comes disguised in the form of misfortune, or temporary defeat."

WHAT IT MEANS NOW:

Most creators start with little money, no product, and a tiny audience. But that struggle forces innovation. Recurring revenue models, digital products, and smart licensing often begin as survival strategies and become million-dollar opportunities. Every asset you build today can earn for you tomorrow, and the next day, and the next.

Most people work like this: They do the task. They get paid. Then they start over again.

That's fine if you want to live on the edge of burnout forever. But if you want time freedom, creative control, and a business that doesn't collapse when you take a day off, you need a different model.

You need to **build once and sell forever**.

THE PROBLEM WITH ONE-TIME WORK

In the traditional model, your income depends on your presence.

No presence = no money

Vacation? Sick day? Burnout? Revenue vanishes.

There's a better way.

When you commit to building a loyal audience over time, you create something far more powerful than a one-time transaction.

You create leverage.

You create it through:

- Content
- Relationships
- Systems
- Trust

And eventually, that turns into **revenue you don't have to chase every day**.

WHAT THE DATA SAYS

- Creators with evergreen digital products earn **2.7x more** than those without (Kit, 2023).

- Most seven-figure creators have **at least five active revenue streams** (Tilt Creator Economy Benchmark study, 2023).

- Once trust is built, loyal audiences can be **800 percent more likely to buy** than cold traffic (River Pools & Spas case study).

Translation? **It pays to stay . . . and to diversify.**

MICHAEL SYMON'S RESTAURANT EMPIRE . . . AND THEN SOME

When most people think of Chef Michael Symon, they picture Cleveland restaurants and Food Network shows. But Michael didn't stop there.

He built a loyal audience and then monetized that trust across:

- Cookbooks

- Licensing deals (airports, stadiums)

- Product lines (knives, sauces)

- Paid media appearances

- Branded merchandise

Each new offer was a new **revenue shelf** he could pull from at any time.

Symon didn't just build a brand. He built a **business model with multiple income lanes**, and it all started with visibility and value.

Symon did one thing. He still does. He makes money from that one thing in dozens of ways.

HOW TO THINK LIKE AN ASSET BUILDER

Here's what successful creators do differently: They don't ask, "What can I sell this week?" They ask, **"What can I build now that I can sell again and again?"**

Think in three layers:

1. **Anchor assets.** These are evergreen pieces that drive consistent value:

    - Courses

    - Books

    - Digital workshops

    - Toolkits

    - Paid newsletters

2. **Promotional pathways.** You need ways to get those assets in front of the right people:

    - Evergreen email sequences

    - High-value lead magnets

    - Speaking appearances

    - Podcast appearances

    - Findable articles

3. **Recurring offers.** The real magic happens when you don't have to restart every month:

    - Memberships

    - Subscriptions

    - Community access

    - Licenses

Each layer builds on the other.

BE LIKE JOHN WICK

The 2014 movie *John Wick* did $43 million at the U.S./Canadian box office that year. It was the 79th ranked movie that year, barely surpassing *Dolphin Tale 2*.

It squeaked out a small profit, and it seemed to find a fan base. Which led to three sequels.

All in all, there is (to date):

- *John Wick* (2014)—$43 million (U.S. and Canada)
- *John Wick Chapter 2* (2017)—$92 million
- *John Wick Chapter 3* (2019)—$171 million
- *John Wick Chapter 4* (2023)—$187 million

Worldwide, the *John Wick* franchise has generated more than $1 billion.

The secret to its success? *Focus+consistency over time.*

John Wick is successful because the story continued. Just think if they would have stopped after the first movie.

Most creators do one thing (a book, an event, a podcast) and expect it to be successful the first time. This rarely, if ever, happens.

Whatever you decide to do with your content, follow the *John Wick* model: **Do one thing well for a specific audience and deliver it consistently over time.**

Bonus: John Grisham's advice for marketing a first book: "Write a second book."

REVENUE RIPPLES

Sometimes the most valuable returns are the **unexpected ones**.

Doug Kessler calls these "ripples." Things like:

- Speaking invites
- High-dollar client inquiries
- Media coverage
- Strategic partnerships

You won't see them coming. But when you build assets and show up consistently, **they will come**.

DIVERSIFICATION OF REVENUE IS SURVIVAL

The best creators have one focus area but make money from that area in dozens of ways.

Whether it's:

- Affiliate programs
- Sponsorships
- Online courses
- Events
- Subscriptions
- Merchandise
- Licensing
- Direct product sales
- Consulting
- Donations

. . . your job isn't to do all of them at once.

It's to build one. Then another. Then another.

Remember: Amazon sold just books for *three* years. Once it was successful with books, it diversified. Today it sells everything. The lesson? Sell one thing first, learn from it, and then move on.

One brick. One shelf. One stream.

Over time, you're not just building income. You're building **resilience**.

Another example: MrBeast (Jimmy Donaldson) is the highest-earning creator on the planet, but he started with one source, YouTube advertising, and grew from there.

As of 2024, MrBeast's business empire includes **at least nine distinct revenue streams**, generating over **$473 million annually** with projections nearing **$1 billion** in 2025 (*Business Insider*).

Here's how he's built a diversified portfolio:

1. **YouTube Ad revenue.** His main channel and spin-offs bring in millions per month from video views.

2. **Feastables.** His ethical chocolate brand topped $215 million in sales, surpassing his media revenue.

3. **Merchandise.** Clothing and branded gear make up around 40 percent of his income.

4. **Sponsorships.** He has long-term partnerships with major brands like Shopify and Amazon.

5. **Amazon Prime show (Beast Games).** He made a nearly $100 million streaming deal that expanded his audience reach.

6. **MrBeast Lab.** He developed a toy and collectibles line that generated $65 million in six months.

7. **Lunchly.** A packaged food brand launched with Logan Paul and KSI, hitting $5 million in 11 weeks.

8. **Software ventures.** These ventures include analytics tools, a creator platform, and upcoming fintech projects.

9. **Philanthropy channels.** His charitable content generates views, engagement, and brand goodwill, while raising millions (#TeamTrees, #TeamSeas).

MrBeast didn't just grow his YouTube presence. He turned audience trust into a **repeatable, diversified revenue engine**.

"You don't need a hundred million followers to do this," he said. "You just need an audience that trusts you and something real to offer" (*Business Insider*).

MEL ROBBINS AND THE THREE LEGS OF THE STOOL

Back when I started in publishing, we used an antiquated strategy called the "three-legged stool." The concept was that in order to be the industry's leading media content provider, we needed to be the **expert provider of information using online, print, and in-person**—the three legs of the stool. In short, it means you were the leading dot-com destination, you had the number one print magazine in your industry, and you had the industry's leading in-person event. Online, print, and in-person.

Funny thing is, this strategy is still the core of success as a content entrepreneur today . . . but it's changed just a little bit.

Let's break it down.

If you look at successful content creators now, they have a modified three legs of the stool that vault them to success.

Mel Robbins is an excellent example of this.

After starting her career as an attorney, she joined CNN as a legal analyst. She parlayed that success into her debut book called *Stop Saying You're Fine* in 2011.

Enter stool leg number one—**the book.**

From that, she started spreading her message through public speaking. In June 2011 her TEDx presentation went viral and has now been viewed more than 33 million times. From that point, Robbins worked as a keynote speaker around the globe, making millions in the process.

Enter stool leg number two—**speaking**.

Good model, right? But it's not great. Not yet. She was missing the third leg of the stool. She needed a regular show.

In 2019, Robbins partnered with Sony Pictures Television for a daytime talk show called *The Mel Robbins Show*. It ran for one season, but it gave her the idea for the third leg.

In 2022, Robbins launched the Mel Robbins Podcast. This is where, two times a week, she creates and distributes a show for millions of listeners to tune into via YouTube or their favorite pod player.

Enter stool leg number three—**the show**.

Your big move could (and maybe should) include this type of model.

What legs of the stool do you already have? What's missing?

Or maybe you have all three, but one of the legs is not pulling its weight (causing your business model to fail).

Take a look and be honest with yourself. If you can't, ask someone in your life who knows your business.

CASE STUDY: EMILY ATKIN—FROM JOURNALIST TO CLIMATE THOUGHT LEADER

When journalist Emily Atkin launched her newsletter *Heated*, she wasn't backed by a major publication or legacy platform. She had an email list, a clear point of view, and a small but loyal audience that cared deeply about climate change.

She chose Substack as her publishing platform and offered *Heated* for $8/month or $75/year.

She didn't need a million followers. She needed a few thousand who believed in the mission and were willing to pay for clarity, research, and insight.

Over time, Emily layered on:

- Speaking gigs
- Brand sponsorships
- Partnerships with nonprofits
- Paid access to special content and tools

She turned deep expertise and consistent publishing into a full-time business **without relying on traditional advertising**.

Start small. Go deep. Build trust. Scale smart.

LET'S GO!

Stop thinking in days and dollars. Start thinking in assets and leverage.

You already have the ideas. Now build the products, the systems, and the shelves that let you scale.

Burn the playbook that says effort equals income. Build once. Sell forever. That's how creators grow free.

CHAPTER 8

THE ALGORITHM IS PATIENCE

(Almost everyone quits too early. Stay long enough to win.)

WHAT HILL SAID/WHAT IT MEANS NOW

WHAT HILL SAID (1937):

> *"One of the most common causes of failure is the habit of quitting when one is overtaken by temporary defeat."*

WHAT IT MEANS NOW:

If you're not willing to be bad at something for a while, you'll never be great at it. The algorithm is patience.

Short steps. Long vision.

—Pitbull

In almost every case, the difference between success and failure isn't talent.

It's patience and persistence. Specifically, **sticking around long enough for your work to catch up to your potential**.

Too many creators quit just before things click. They stop publishing right before the trust kicks in. They shift strategy right before the results compound.

They walk away on day 180 . . . when day 181 is when everything was about to happen.

This chapter is about making sure you don't do that.

"Nothing in the world can take the place of persistence. Talent will not; nothing is more common than unsuccessful men with talent. Genius will not; unrewarded genius is almost a proverb. Education will not; the world is full of educated derelicts. Persistence and determination alone are omnipotent. The slogan 'Press On' has solved and always will solve the problems of the human race."

—*Calvin Coolidge, 30th President of the United States (1923–1929)*

THE UNSEXY TRUTH ABOUT SUCCESS

Success rarely looks like a single breakthrough.

It looks like:

- Showing up when no one replies
- Publishing when the metrics are flat
- Believing when the dopamine is gone
- Saying "Not yet" instead of "This didn't work"

Momentum isn't flashy. It's invisible . . . until it's not.

"Most people overestimate what they can do in one year and underestimate what they can do in ten."

—Bill Gates

WHAT THE DATA SAYS

- In the Tilt Creator Economy Benchmark study, most creators who achieve full-time income levels do so **in years, not months.**

- A HubSpot analysis of blogging performance showed that **over 90 percent of leads come from posts published at least three months earlier**, not recent content.

- In the world of content findability, the average time for content to hit peak ranking? **Six to twelve months.**

Trust, discovery, and authority don't operate on your personal timeline. They operate on **consistency and volume.**

DARREN ROWSE—BLOGGING THROUGH THE DIP

Darren Rowse launched *Digital Photography School* (DPS) in 2006.

For the first two years, the blog barely moved. Traffic trickled in. Revenue was inconsistent. There were no viral moments, no overnight successes. Just post after post, week after week.

But he stuck with it.

Today *DPS* generates millions in revenue through e-books, courses, affiliate income, and sponsorships. The archives span thousands of tutorials and product reviews, and the audience returns because the content is *that good.*

It took time. It took trust. It took staying long enough to matter.

THE COMPOUND EFFECT OF TRUST

Here's what staying power actually builds:

1. **Skill.** Your voice gets stronger. Your work gets sharper.

2. **Visibility.** Algorithms and audiences favor consistency.

3. **Credibility.** People trust the ones who *don't disappear.*

4. **Opportunity.** Long-term content builds surface area for good things to find you (partnerships, press, invitations).

Success isn't a straight line. It's a **staircase hidden in a fog.** You don't see the next step until you take the one in front of you.

WHAT TO DO WHEN IT'S NOT WORKING (YET)

1. **Audit the work, not your worth.** If something's not landing, adjust the format, not your identity.

2. **Talk to your audience.** Ask what they're struggling with. Often the breakthrough is in *listening*, not pivoting.

3. **Reduce complexity.** Go back to your Tilt. One message, one channel, one product. Then refine from there.

4. **Take one small step per day.** Publishing daily? Keep going. Posting weekly? Stay on schedule.

Don't scale back when you feel stuck. *Simplify and stay the course.*

When I came to the crossroads in 2009, I decided to review all my blog comments (again) to see what readers were saying. I didn't notice the first time, but there was a pattern. Readers were asking for training and in-person events. Two years later we premiered Content Marketing World, and the rest was history.

The point? Listening to your audience's needs and desires is always a smart move.

SELL SO YOU CAN STAY IN THE GAME

When I launched my content business, I didn't have a reliable revenue stream. The plan was to build an audience first, then monetize. But with a growing family at home and no revenue coming in, we needed income *immediately*, not months from then.

So, while building the long game, I took on consulting work. One client, a nonprofit serving mechanical engineers, had a problem: its ad revenue was cratering and digital sales were failing. The client had little website traffic, no digital sales strategy, and a sales team that didn't understand how to pitch online ads.

We didn't have time to wait for more traffic. People were about to lose jobs.

So we introduced something new: a **limited-inventory sponsorship model**. Instead of selling endless banner ads to a tiny audience (which wasn't working), we flipped the script:

- We sold just **six sponsorships per month**.
- Each sponsor was labeled a "partner" and received exclusive logo placements.
- Scarcity drove value. We increased prices significantly.
- Sponsors were offered category exclusivity at a premium.

The sales team hated it . . . at first. But within a week, we sold out the entire sponsorship model for six months. Revenue spiked by over 500 percent. That model became the blueprint for all future digital sales, including webinars, directories, and white papers.

And I kept the model in mind.

THE BENEFACTOR PIVOT

By 2009, my own business was in trouble. We had cut expenses to the bone, but we were bleeding cash. Our core product wasn't scaling fast enough, and I was close to walking away.

Then I remembered the limited-inventory model.

So we created the **Benefactor Package**: a premium sponsorship model for just 10 companies that wanted to support our mission. Each benefactor got exposure to our audience and the ability to contribute content.

We sold out of inventory. It gave us the cash to pivot to what became the Content Marketing Institute. A year later, we made the Inc. 500 list of fastest-growing companies.

Moral of the story: To stay in the game **you need to sell**. Early and often.

You don't need a perfect product. You need a simple offer, a clear ask, and the confidence to say, *"This is what we're doing. Are you in?"*

I hate to say this, but the reality is that many creators who struggle aren't selling enough. You need to make the calls, adjust based on feedback, and call again.

THE TALE OF TWO TREES

Once, in a quiet valley, two saplings took root side by side . . . one a silver maple, the other an oak.

The maple shot up quickly. Each day, it stretched higher toward the sun, its leaves bright and boastful.

The oak, meanwhile, grew slowly. It sank its roots deep into the soil, twisting around rocks, anchoring itself one inch at a time.

Seasons passed. The maple grew tall and wide, basking in praise from birds and breezes. The oak remained modest: shorter, quieter, unnoticed.

Then one autumn, a great storm swept through the valley. The wind howled and the rain pummeled the earth. The maple, with all its height and beauty, had never faced a trial like this. Its roots, shallow and untested, couldn't hold. With a final groan, it toppled to the ground.

The oak stood firm.

In the silence after the storm, the valley looked different. The oak, once overshadowed, now reached the light. Not because it grew the fastest, but because it grew the strongest.

This story is true both in biology and as a metaphor.

Many fast-growing trees like silver maples, willows, and some poplars tend to have shallow root systems. They shoot up quickly but lack deep anchoring. In contrast, slow-growing trees like oaks invest in deep roots early. When a storm comes, shallow-rooted trees are the first to fall.

The lesson? The longer you take to achieve success, the better for your long-term success. You'll be able to survive longer if you don't hit instant success. Just ask Haliey Welch (Hawk Tuah Girl), Laina Morris (Overly Attached Girlfriend), Danielle Bregoli (Bhad Bhabie), or Fredo Santana (SoundCloud Era). You can look it up.

LET'S GO!

Staying is hard. It's also what separates the pros from the tourists.

You don't need another plan. You need to keep walking the path you're on.

Burn the playbook that says success should be fast. Stay until it works. Because that's when it really starts to matter.

"Everything is impossible until it happens."

—Nelson Mandela

CHAPTER 9

CURATE YOUR CREW

(Build your Board of Life to grow faster and last longer.)

WHAT HILL SAID/WHAT IT MEANS NOW

WHAT HILL SAID (1937):

> *"No individual has sufficient experience, education, native ability, and knowledge to ensure the accumulation of a great fortune, without the cooperation of other people."*

WHAT IT MEANS NOW:

You don't need a big team. You need the *right* voices at your side. Your personal advisory board matters more than your follower count.

You don't build a business alone.

You can try. And for a while, it might work. But the moment things get hard (and they always do) you'll either have people to lean on . . . or collapse under the weight of your own ambition.

Whom you surround yourself with is one of the biggest factors in whether you grow or burn out.

That's why this chapter isn't about networking. It's about **curation**.

The best creators build a Board of Life . . . an intentional group of people who:

- Challenge their thinking

- Hold them accountable

- Remind them who they are

- Celebrate when things finally break through

It's time to build yours.

THE PROBLEM WITH GOING IT ALONE

Entrepreneurship can be lonely. Even more so when you're doing something unconventional, like content-first business building.

Without a crew:

- Impostor syndrome grows louder.

- Bad ideas echo with no one to filter them.

- Opportunities pass by because you're too buried in your own head.

And worst of all, there's no one to tell you **to keep going when it gets boring, painful, or slow.**

WHAT THE DATA SAYS

- According to Harvard research, people with strong personal and professional support systems are **2–3x more likely** to reach major career goals.

- Founders with regular peer feedback grow their businesses **30 percent faster** than those who isolate (SCORE Foundation, 2023).

- One study showed that 70 percent of entrepreneurs struggle with mental health challenges; yet those with at least one accountability partner report **50 percent lower burnout levels**.

Support isn't soft. It's **strategic infrastructure**.

THE FIVE ROLES EVERY CREATOR NEEDS

You don't need a cast of thousands. You just need a few of these voices in your corner:

1. **The truth teller.** The person who calls your bluff. They'll tell you when you're playing small or avoiding the hard stuff.

2. **The superfan.** The person who reminds you why your work matters, especially on the days when *you* forget.

3. **The expert.** Someone further along who shares what works and what doesn't so you don't have to learn everything the hard way.

4. **The peer.** A fellow creator in the arena with you. They get the grind. You can swap notes, vent, and grow together.

5. **The connector.** Someone who opens doors, makes introductions, and sees potential you haven't tapped yet.

You don't need one person to be all five. You just need to **intentionally surround yourself with people who make you better**.

Of course, you can try to do it alone, but I've rarely seen it happen. It's okay to ask for help. And the funny thing? There are people in your life who truly want to help you and see you succeed. **Remember . . . they need this too.**

CASE STUDY: THE QUIET POWER OF COLLABORATION

This Old Marketing is a podcast I started with Robert Rose back in 2013. Today it's one of the most popular content marketing podcasts in the world. When we started, we didn't have a big plan. We had conversations we wanted to have . . . and a shared belief in content as a business driver.

What we didn't realize at the time was that our back-and-forth, our structure, and our consistency would lead to:

- Deeper ideas

- Stronger reach

- Real friendship

- And business deals we never could've closed alone

The show worked not just because of the content. It worked because we challenged and elevated each other every week.

If you're trying to do everything solo, you're leaving growth on the table.

In his book *Sponsor Magnet*, Justin Moore talks about the power of working directly with brands to take your business to the next level. But Justin has taken that one step further and suggests that entrepreneurs should work with others not only to build audience, but to drive direct revenue.

If you're stuck doing either by yourself, try partnering with someone on the outside who shares your goals and audience.

WHAT IF YOUR CREW DOESN'T EXIST YET?

Then you build one.

Here's how:

- Join a mastermind.
- Ask someone you admire for a 30-minute chat.
- Hire a coach or mentor.
- Start a private group with two or three creators in your space.
- Attend one in-person event this year with the goal of *meeting your people*.

This isn't about networking for business cards. It's about building a bench.

ON BUILDING COMMUNITY

When I decided to create the event Content Entrepreneur Expo (CEX), we developed a VIP group to be the backbone. 75 people raised their hand to come together for regular meetings, meetups at CEX, and submeetings to support each other. This group organized and wrote the book *The Content Entrepreneur*, and several members of the group continue to help each other on their individual creator journeys through weekly meetings and shared goals. It's truly powerful.

Drew McLellan, founder of Agency Management Institute, believes in this so much he added it to his company mission: **We get better faster by learning with and from each other**. Drew's advice to entrepreneurs is to "build a community around you of the people you serve so they can be of service to one another as well."

Finding your crew is important, even critical, but if you can build a community that helps each other in the process, you won't build anything more powerful. It could be as simple as hosting a mastermind, hosting a group on Discord, or participating in group coaching.

DO WHAT YOU DO WELL AND OUTSOURCE THE REST

A few years after starting my business, I began to make mistakes. Specifically, I was terrible at scheduling and started dropping the ball on other details.

I was pretty good at strategy and horrible at the day-to-day of making things work.

I asked my wife for help. From that moment on, not only did she take over my calendar, but she took over operations for the entire company. As you know, this worked to perfection.

This will work for you as well.

The first step is to create a list. On one side, list all the things you love to do or are good at. On the other side, list all the things you hate to do or are bad at.

Keep all the good things. Outsource all the bad things.

Sometimes you'll need just one person. Other times, you'll need dozens of people doing a few hours of work in a week for you.

Smart business.

WHY YOU NEED TO BE CHALLENGED

It was the day before I ran my first-ever marathon.

My wife and I were in Toledo (Ohio) sitting inside a Whole Foods. I was talking to her about my marathon thoughts. I was a bit jumpy. Anxious about the next day. She asked if I had a time goal. I told her that all the advice I received was not to have a time goal. Just finish. Finishing is enough.

I sensed she wanted to say something. Her complexion changed a bit; then she laid it on me.

In so many words, she said that wasn't good enough. That I'd done the work. To a tee I'd done the work. I skipped two runs because of injury over the past four months, but other than that I hit every run. I ran in the Bahamas. I got up early to run on our family vacation. I ran 60 laps around a cruise ship . . . two times, mind you. I ran 22 miles around the west side of London, England.

Then she asked, "Don't you have a time goal? Are you a Pulizzi?"

Now, when she brings out the "Are you a Pulizzi?", that always gets my attention. As you already know, we are "Go big or go home" people. She was challenging me. I decided to do this thing . . . and made the decision to do just this one marathon. And since I was making this decision, how was I not going to go all out?

I was mad. More than mad—I was pissed. Then I started to rationalize. I showed her my splits for my other training runs. My fastest mile splits, for any of my runs, were around 9:30 (9 minutes 30 seconds). My runs over 15 miles were around 10:30 to 11 or higher. I said, how could I run much faster than 4:30 when nothing I've done showed me I could?

The number she thought I could do was 4:15. I ran my last half marathon in 2:07, so she said to just double that. "You should just do that," she said. I told her it wasn't that easy.

We went to bed early, and I stayed awake for a while thinking ("stewing" might be the better word). I was obsessed over what she said. Was I settling? Was I just taking the advice of others because that's the way most people did it?

The race the next day was to start at 6:30 a.m. Around 5:30 a.m. I had some alone time to drink my coffee and stretch, and I made the decision to go all out. I would start the first mile at a nice pace, around 10 . . . then work to get a little faster for each mile until about halfway, and then hold on for dear life.

Mile 1 I did in 9:58. Perfect start.

At mile 8 I hit a 9:04 split.

I hit my lowest split at mile 9 with an 8:55.

I kept on with all my miles under 10 minutes until mile 22 and hit the proverbial wall. I hung on and finished at 4 hours and 15 minutes.

Here's what I learned:

First, it's okay to take advice, but turn all that advice into your own decision and actually make it your own.

Second, we only live once, so whatever you decide to do, give it everything you've got.

I'm sure if I had come in at 4:29, I would still be happy that I finished my first marathon, but I couldn't honestly say that I gave everything physically and mentally to the task.

Third, listen to the members of your crew. If you do this correctly, those are the people who will be honest with you no matter what.

After the race, I was walking back, hand in hand with my wife. She was smiling because she knew. And I thanked her. I told her I was mad at her, and I thanked her for what she said, because it was right. She said that's why we are perfect for each other: "You challenge me as well. We are supposed to make each other better."

THE HARD TRUTH

As you make your crew decisions, you need to realize some things:

- You might not have any family members as part of your crew.
- You might lose some friendships that you've had since the beginning. It's unfortunate but true.
- You'll get to a point, probably when you are close to real success, that the mix of people you hang around will have to change. The path you choose may not include a few people that got you to this point.

LET'S GO!

You were never meant to do this alone.

Find the people who sharpen your vision. Build your Board of Life. Then trust them enough to help carry the weight when it's heavy.

Burn the playbook that says independence means isolation. Great creators curate the people who help them go further and stay longer.

CHAPTER 10

THE UNDISCOVERED COUNTRIES

(There are underserved audiences in plain sight.)

WHAT HILL SAID/WHAT IT MEANS NOW

WHAT HILL SAID (1937):

"It is literally true that you can succeed best and quickest by helping others to succeed."

WHAT IT MEANS NOW:

In a world obsessed with visibility, the real edge is in *relevance*. Serving an overlooked audience doesn't just make you useful. It makes you indispensable. While others chase popularity, you build trust. Trust leads to loyalty. Loyalty leads to revenue. The path to freedom doesn't run through the masses. It runs through the margins.

WHERE THE REAL OPPORTUNITIES ARE

If you're serious about escaping the system and building something you own, this is the moment to look where no one else is looking. Most entrepreneurs chase saturated markets. Most creators target the obvious audiences. But what if the real opportunity, the Tilt worth owning, is hiding in plain sight?

REALITY BITES

My friend and I did a little experiment with some younger adults in our lives, from our own children to our friends' kids. Most recently graduated from college. Here's a list of their education and specialty areas and where they are currently working:

- Retail management. At a large clothing retailer
- IT support. Call center and in-person IT support for a bank
- Psychology. Working toward psychology practice
- Nursing. In a hospital
- Teaching. In a public school system
- Healthcare research. For a mid-size university
- Software engineering. For a tech company in California

If these roles are around in five years, they will be drastically different. With automation and cashless checkout, retail management is challenging. IT support is being wiped out by AI-powered help desks and chatbots. Psychology is quickly moving to AI therapy channels. For nursing, robotic support is on the way. For teaching, the educational system is currently going through a defunded revolution. And while healthcare research needs human oversight, many of the former research roles are gone for good.

Who really knows where things will go? No one.

But one thing is for sure. As we all learn new skills, or drastically evolve the roles we currently have, do we want to find a cog in the system that will accept us or do we want to build something where we can be flexible to the world's demands?

Even if the titles still exist, **the jobs will not look the same**. The people who win are not the most credentialed but the most **curious, visible**, and **adaptive**.

In a world of accelerating automation, *building your own system* is the only safe bet.

Right now in America, entire groups of people are desperate for guidance, tools, and connection. They are underserved not because they're small, but because they've been overlooked. And that's where you come in.

Here are six groups with massive unmet needs and how you can step in, serve them, and build a powerful, profitable business around it:

1. OLDER ADULTS (THE "SILVER TSUNAMI")

- **Why they're overlooked**. By 2034, Americans over 65 will outnumber children. Many still lack broadband, tech skills, and tailored health resources. Twenty-two million seniors have no broadband at home. Most digital platforms simply aren't designed with them in mind.

- **Tilt opportunity**. Build tech literacy content for seniors. Create simplified tools or offer concierge-style digital services for families. Think online Medicare navigation, voice-first apps, or "grandkid-proof" video chat setups.

- **Proof point**. AT&T has committed $5 billion since 2021 toward digital equity including programs aimed at seniors.

Tilt It: Be the translator. Seniors don't need new tech. They need trusted guides to help them use tech that already exists.

2. NEW ENTREPRENEURS AND SIDE HUSTLERS

- **Why they're overlooked.** The United States is in an entrepreneurship boom, with 5.5 million new business applications in 2023 alone. But 42 percent of businesses fail because there's no market need, and 82 percent cite cash flow issues. These aren't just failures. They're signals of unmet educational needs.

- **Tilt opportunity.** Serve solo creators, part-time founders, or non-tech entrepreneurs. Offer content like "Finance 101 for Creators," "Legal Checklists for Etsy Sellers," or coaching for rural or minority entrepreneurs starting with zero network.

- **Proof point.** More than 25 percent of small businesses can't get the funding they need. This creates an opening for education, microloans, and community-focused advisory services.

Tilt It: You don't have to invent the next Uber. Just help overlooked founders take their first real step.

3. SMALL B2B AND INDUSTRIAL BUSINESSES

- **Why they're overlooked.** B2B firms make up 98 percent of U.S. manufacturers, but only a small percentage use AI. Many don't have IT departments, digital marketing, or even basic e-commerce capability.

- **Tilt opportunity.** Start a blog or YouTube channel simplifying digital transformation. Offer tools like a "mini ERP" for small factories. Provide plain-English guides for compliance, AI, or automation. Or build peer networks to help small operators share resources.

- **Proof point.** These firms could boost productivity by 26–50 percent with the right tech, but they don't know where to start.

Tilt It: Be the "digital whisperer" for the blue-collar B2B world. Speak their language. Show up consistently.

4. EMERGING TECH USERS (EARLY ADOPTERS WITHOUT A MAP)

- **Why they're overlooked**. Millions are diving into AI, crypto, or smart tech without a clear roadmap. Over 63 percent of Americans don't trust crypto's safety. Early adopters often end up overwhelmed, scammed, or stuck.

- **Tilt opportunity**. Create a guide for parents trying to understand AI. Start a podcast about the use of responsible wearables for schools. Launch a platform for AI use cases that avoid hype and focus on utility. Help creators navigate copyright in the age of generative content.

- **Proof point**. ChatGPT hit 100 million users in two months. But how many are using it well? There's massive space for interpretation and support.

Tilt It: Today's tech is moving faster than comprehension. Translate complexity into clarity.

5. RURAL AND REMOTE COMMUNITIES

- **Why they're overlooked**. Sixty million Americans live in rural areas. Twenty-eight percent lack broadband. Hundreds of rural hospitals have closed. Local news has disappeared in over two hundred counties.

- **Tilt opportunity**. Launch a newsletter or podcast just for a rural niche. Help farmers adopt agri-tech. Build community information hubs or health navigation tools. As rural newspapers dry up, help the local population keep track of important news.

- **Proof point.** At one time, the BEAD federal program was investing $42 billion to close the rural broadband gap. But infrastructure without guidance won't be enough.

Tilt It: You don't have to be rural to serve rural. Be the bridge.

6. ENERGY (THE INFRASTRUCTURE NO ONE SEES)

- **Why it's overlooked**. Every new technology (including AI, data centers, electric vehicles, crypto, and smart homes) runs on power. A lot of it. But while innovation gets headlines, the infrastructure that supports it often goes ignored. As demand surges, the world is heading straight into an energy bottleneck.

- Nuclear power, once written off, is making a quiet comeback. So are microgrids, smart energy systems, and alternative fuels. But there's a major gap: The general public doesn't understand what's happening, and local communities, schools, and small businesses are totally unprepared.

- **Tilt opportunity**. Become the translator, educator, or guide in the energy space:

  ◦ Start a YouTube channel explaining nuclear myths versus facts.

  ◦ Launch a newsletter on "future-proof energy" for homeowners or schools.

  ◦ Offer courses for young professionals who want careers in renewables.

  ◦ Help those moving from technology and coding (which AI is taking over) figure out how to transfer knowledge to this "new" type of engineering.

- ○ Create content around how creators and small businesses can prep for the energy demands of digital work and AI tools.

- **Proof point.** The U.S. Department of Energy projects that electricity demand could grow **up to 38 percent by 2035**, driven largely by data centers and electric vehicles. Meanwhile, the nuclear energy workforce is shrinking.

Tilt It: Energy is the most urgent and invisible opportunity of the next decade. You don't need to be an engineer. You just need to explain what's coming and help people make smarter decisions now.

HELP FIRST. MONETIZE LATER

Here's the common thread across all these groups: People need **guidance before they buy**. They need **trust before they transact**. That means your content is the business . . . at least to start.

First, **show up consistently.** Second, **solve a real problem.** Then, **offer the paid product or service.**

And as Scott Galloway says, "The less sexy an industry, the greater return on your capital." Be mindful of that.

This is how the best businesses are built today, from Substack creators to SaaS founders. You build the audience first, serve their needs, and earn permission to make the sale.

The "playbook" says chase broad markets and scale fast. We say start small, go deep, and serve well.

DISCOVERING YOUR WORTHY CAUSE?

Marcus Sheridan says that whenever his kids get down on themselves or their current situation, he asks them one simple question: *"What is your worthy cause right now?"*

Marcus went on to talk about when content creators get down on their business, or when people get depressed, in many cases it's because they don't have a cause that is meaningful. **To Marcus, a meaningful cause or purpose is something that helps the world and the person at the same time**.

That resonates with me. I often felt lost after becoming an entrepreneur. I was creating all this content about content marketing to get search traffic for my business, but there wasn't a deep mission. I was flailing.

Then I realized there was a large group of marketers that didn't understand the practice of content marketing, and needed to, to get and keep jobs, to be fulfilled, to support their families. They needed it for career survival.

We took on the mission to help teach the "how-to" behind content marketing because we believed the industry didn't just want it. They needed it. We believed it was a worthy cause. And at the same time, we believed that a worthy cause could create significant business for our family.

It was like turning on a light switch. I went from being listless and, frankly, almost giving up on the whole idea of being an entrepreneur, to being excited to get up each morning.

What is your worthy cause right now? What gets *you* up in the morning? What are *you* doing today to help people and yourself?

So when I asked the question, "Marcus, what would you say to content entrepreneurs who are really struggling right now?" He said, without skipping a beat, that the most important thing we can do as content creators is to have purpose in our life and business. Without that one thing, you probably won't be successful.

Do you know your purpose? If someone asked, could you recite it?

If you're not sure, write down a best guess. Play with it for a while. You're on this earth now for a reason . . . maybe your worthy cause hasn't been discovered quite yet. But you'll get there.

FINAL WORD

One of the reasons I wrote *Content Inc.* was because of people like Andy Schneider. Meeting him changed my life.

Andy Schneider built an entire business around one overlooked question: *"How do I raise backyard chickens?"*

While the rest of the world was teaching SEO or personal finance, Andy launched a podcast, wrote books, hosted a magazine, and toured the country speaking to hobby farmers and suburban chicken owners. Yes . . . chicken owners.

Although he's retired from the limelight, he's still known nationally as the *"Chicken Whisperer,"* racking up sponsorships, speaking gigs, and large media deals over the years . . . not because he went mainstream, but because he went weird and specific.

If you're looking for your Tilt, your niche, your category, your moment, it may not be in the hot trends or the crowded spaces.

It may be in the corners. In the gaps. In the underserved.

That's not charity. That's strategy.

And the most satisfying kind of success? The kind that helps someone else win first.

LET'S GO!

You don't need a massive market. You need a meaningful one.

Serve the ones no one else sees. Show up where others overlook.

Burn the playbook that says success is scale. Real growth starts in the margins.

CHAPTER 11

YOUR FU FINANCIAL POSITION

(The ultimate freedom isn't money. It's the power to walk away.)

WHAT HILL SAID/WHAT IT MEANS NOW

WHAT HILL SAID (1937):

> *"Money without brains is always dangerous.*
> *Properly used, it is the most important essential of freedom."*

WHAT IT MEANS NOW:

Freedom isn't just about having money. It's about what that money lets you say no to. A true FU financial position gives you control over your time, your decisions, and your future. It's not wealth for show; it's wealth that works for you when it matters most.

Here's the truth I've learned over the past 30 years: **It's nearly impossible to make a real impact on the world if you don't have control over how you spend your time**. It really is that simple.

And there's one moment in one movie that reminds me of this more than anything else.

I've never been able to watch *The Gambler* with Mark Wahlberg and John Goodman all the way through. The downward spiral of Wahlberg's character, drowning in debt and desperation, hits a little too close to home.

But there's a scene near the end of the film that I've watched more than 100 times. It's the moment when Wahlberg's character, Jim Bennett, goes to borrow a large sum of money from Frank, the no-nonsense loan shark played by Goodman.

Before Frank agrees to the loan, he delivers this monologue:

Frank:

"You get up two and a half million dollars, anyone in the world knows what to do:

You get a house with a 25-year roof.

An indestructible Jap-economy sh*tbox.

You put the rest into the system at three to five percent to pay your taxes and that's your base. That's your fortress of solitude.

That puts you, for the rest of your life, at a level of FU.

Somebody wants you to do something—FU.

Boss pisses you off—FU.

Own your house.

Have a couple bucks in the bank.

Don't drink.

That's all I have to say to anybody on any social level."

Frank calls it the **FU position**, and he's absolutely right.

But here's the part people miss: **The FU position isn't about money**.

It's about **leverage**. It's about **freedom**. It's about never again being stuck saying *yes* because you *have* to.

THE POWER OF THE FU POSITION

The FU position is when you can:

- Walk away from bad clients
- Turn down shady partnerships
- Say no to jobs, projects, or offers that don't align with your purpose

Not because you're arrogant. Because you're *free*.

And freedom comes from owning three things:

1. Your **income**
2. Your **attention**
3. Your **time**

You don't need millions to get there.

You just need a few simple systems and the will to stick to them.

DO THE FINANCIAL WORK NOW. BE FREE LATER

Financial literacy isn't taught in school. But it can be learned.

Ever wonder why so many lottery winners end up losing it all? Simply put, if you don't have the skills to keep your money, you're bound to keep losing it.

Here's what too many people are still doing:

- Carrying credit card debt (you'll never make more in the market than you are being charged by credit card companies)
- Taking out second and third mortgages
- Ignoring Roth IRAs and tax-free compounding
- Failing to set up wills and trusts

And then . . . something happens. And families get stuck picking up the pieces.

Don't let that be you. Here's your 30-day FU checklist:

1. Spend less than you make.
2. Pay off credit card balances monthly.
3. Open and contribute to a Roth IRA.
4. Update or create your will.
5. Buy a used, not new, car.
6. Make extra principal payments (don't borrow against your house).
7. Build a 90-day emergency fund.
8. Before buying something, ask if you can borrow it first (for example, use the library).

Nail these, and you'll sleep better. You'll work smarter. And if something happens, you've just put your family in a **manageable position. Not a crisis.**

"You will spend 40,000 hours, maybe 60,000 hours of your life trying to make money. I think you should be spending at least 100 hours figuring out how you keep it."

—Michael Saylor, Bitcoin Evangelist

WHAT THE DATA SAYS

Nearly **78 percent of Americans live paycheck to paycheck** (Bureau of Labor Statistics).

Owners pay significantly less in taxes (as a percentage) than earners (Brookings).

True FU freedom comes not from flashy income, but from **sustainable systems**.

CASE STUDY: NATHAN TANKUS—FINANCIAL CONTROL WITHOUT A DEGREE

Nathan Tankus didn't have a traditional career. No degree. No job offers. But he had one thing: clarity on his Tilt.

So he launched *Notes on the Crises*, a paid Substack newsletter.

He acquired 450 subscribers at $1,000/year. That's $450,000 in annual revenue from one voice, one list, and one idea.

He bought back his time. Took control of his work. And now operates from a place of true freedom. On his terms.

WHAT MAKES A MILLIONAIRE?

According to *Entrepreneur* magazine, most people make money in very few ways. Individuals who collect a salary from a business generally have one or maybe two sources of income (their paycheck and possibly an investment account). Perhaps you know many people in this situation. They go to the same job every day, work to pay off their bills, and don't have much left for savings or investment after each month.

Millionaires, on the other hand, have multiple sources of revenue coming in, whether that's through multiple businesses (and multiple products and services within those businesses), real estate transactions, countless investments, or more.

Think about your situation. It doesn't matter what you do, but it does matter how many sources of revenue you have. As you already know, the most successful content entrepreneurs have five, six, seven, plus more different revenue channels.

Before we sold Content Marketing Institute in 2016, most people thought all our revenue came from our event, Content Marketing World, in the form of attendee fees and sponsorships. At that time, we also generated a significant amount through consulting fees, paid email rental, digital sponsorships, webinar programs, and even book sales.

The formula is about being focused on your content and distribution, and being diverse with how you bring in revenue.

Tony Robbins says that the most important financial decision of your life is whether to become an owner and not just a consumer. He states, "You'll never earn your way to financial fortune." You need to own it.

My take? The worst days of my entrepreneurial life have been better than the best days of my life working for someone else.

BUILD YOUR FU BASE

You don't need to be rich to be free. You need:

- **Runway.** Three to six months of cash in the bank
- **Cash flow.** Multiple revenue channels, not just a paycheck
- **Restraint.** A lifestyle that doesn't inflate every time your income does
- **Strategy.** A long-term plan that includes asset building, not just bills

DON'T OVERCOMPLICATE IT

I've been in and around the financial world for over 30 years. I've done it all. Stocks, bonds, options (puts and calls), crypto. I've invested in start-ups, bought and sold companies, and have owned three houses.

When I first started, I overcomplicated everything . . . always looking for that breakout stock and putting more of my eggs in one basket, taking unnecessary risk.

Here's the truth. If you don't have time, or don't want to make time, to really understand how a company makes its money, don't buy its stock.

Get rid of all the complexity. Take 15 percent of what you make each month, put it in a Roth IRA, and invest that money into a low-cost stock market index fund like Vanguard's Total Stock Market (VTSAX).

That's it. As Frank would say, that's your fortress of solitude.

Warren Buffett and Charlie Munger became billionaires not by picking the best companies, but by staying in the market, investing regularly, and waiting. Each of them made 99 percent of their total worth *after* they turned 60.

All that is true and I believe it to my core. If your financial strategy keeps you awake at night, something is wrong; so keep it simple.

That said, as our family has grown our nest egg, we've strategically moved money to create even more diversity.

Diversification might not necessarily give you huge returns, but it does ensure that you sleep at night, and it will grow your hard-earned dollars over time. Our current portfolio looks something like this:

- **U.S. stockholdings, diversified by cap and sector**—45 percent
- **Bitcoin/Ethereum/Solana/Digital Art**—15 percent
- **International stockholdings, diversified by country/region**—10 percent

- **Cash/cash equivalents**—10 percent
- **Bonds, diversified by location and structure**—5 percent
- **Real estate**—5 percent
- **Charity**—5 percent
- **Hedge funds**—5 percent

I am not a qualified investment advisor. I am speaking only from my personal experience. Please seek out qualified help when you are ready.

HOW TO KNOW IT'S TIME TO EXIT

Most people think they'll "just know" when it's time to exit. They're wrong. The signs are subtle at first. Then all at once.

The time to create an exit is always "now." You want to be prepared when the opportunity arises.

Here are a few signals that it might be time to sell, step back, or pivot:

1. **You've hit your freedom number.** Your financial goals are met, and continuing at full pace feels like greed, not purpose. That's a clue.

   My wife and I had a freedom number of $15 million. When the business was worth more than that, we were ready to make our exit.

2. **The mission has shifted.** If what excited you in year one now feels like a grind and your curiosity is pulling elsewhere, it's worth listening.

3. **You've become the bottleneck.** If everything runs through you, and you feel like a glorified email sorter, you don't own a business. You own a job.

4. **The business is worth more to someone else than to you.** If the strategic value is high (brand, audience, recurring revenue) and

you're not energized to grow it further, selling your business might create more leverage than keeping it.

Pro tip: Keep a list of people and companies that would be interested in buying your business. Be sure to keep in touch with them.

5. **You're starting to dream about what's next.** Not in a guilty, escapist way, but in an energized, creative way. Your subconscious is sending a signal.

Reminder: Selling doesn't mean failure. It means completion. And sometimes the best way to grow is to let go. Every life has multiple chapters. It's okay to end one and start another.

Ask yourself, "If someone gave me a check today, what would I do next?"

If that answer excites you more than your current grind, start preparing your exit, even if it's 12–24 months away.

You don't have to escape in crisis. You can exit with clarity.

MAKING THE IMPORTANT DECISIONS

British comedian Jimmy Carr gave an amazing interview with *Diary of a CEO* host Steven Bartlett.

Jimmy recalls a story of a very successful man. Head of a business. A multimillionaire. The man was unhappy because he had worked all the way through his son's childhood. He hadn't bonded with his son and built the kind of relationship he wanted.

He'd been away on business too long. I'm sure you have heard of the type.

The man went to see a psychiatrist and vowed to give up his job. He promised that, in five years, he would leave everything to spend more time with his child. He would not do any more work and would focus on his son.

The man did it. He was very happy and had no regrets. He decided to live in that moment.

That man was John Lennon of the Beatles. That kid was Sean Lennon.

Jimmy goes on to say that no matter how important you think your job is, you aren't John Lennon. I'm sure Lennon could have done great things musically in those five years, but look at the gift he created and gave to his son.

John Lennon made the decision to give up everything in business to spend time with his family.

No one knows for sure but I bet John Lennon didn't regret that decision, one that seems especially consequential in light of the fact that his life was tragically cut short a few years later. I bet Sean believes this was the right decision as well.

Here's the point: He didn't put it off. Something was not right. He was unhappy. He made the decision. He didn't say he'd do it in a year, or after the next album, or after the next tour. He dropped everything to do something he believed was most important. Because he had the freedom to make it happen.

He did it. So can you.

Be John Lennon.

LET'S GO!

Freedom isn't a number in your bank account. It's waking up and choosing how you spend your time.

Build your base. Build your systems. And when someone asks you to compromise, **you'll have the leverage to say no.**

Burn the playbook that says freedom is a dream. The real power move is the FU position. And it's available to you sooner than you think.

PART IV

LIVING DIFFERENT, LIVING BETTER

CHAPTER 12

PROTECT YOUR FEED

(What you consume shapes what you become.)

WHAT HILL SAID/WHAT IT MEANS NOW

WHAT HILL SAID (1937):

"Control your own mind, and you may never be controlled by the mind of another."

WHAT IT MEANS NOW:

Your mental operating system needs boundaries. In the age of algorithmic distraction, attention is everything, and most people give it away without even noticing.

If you don't intentionally protect your mind from the constant stream of noise, conflict, and anxiety-inducing clickbait, your goals will get hijacked. Your mental bandwidth will evaporate.

You already know that:

- Social media is addicting.
- News is designed to inflame, not inform.
- "Urgent" alerts are rarely urgent.

But here's the real risk: **Every piece of content you consume is programming you**.

As we've learned, your brain is always listening.

Which means if you want to live free, think clearly, and act with intention, you need to **curate your feed like your future depends on it**.

Because it does.

THE INVISIBLE COST OF NOISE

You only get so many quality thinking hours per day.

And most people waste them reacting to things that don't matter:

- Angry Twitter/X threads
- Random YouTube drama
- Constant Slack or Discord messages
- Group chats that never stop buzzing
- Phone notifications that never end

Every distraction has a cost:

- Lost focus
- Decreased ability to go deep on your own ideas

And every "little scroll" adds up.

The feed you don't control will eventually control you.

WHAT THE DATA SAYS

- According to the American Psychological Association, **constant media exposure is one of the top three contributors to chronic anxiety**.

- The average adult checks their phone **144 times per day** and spends over **4 hours** on social media (*PCMag*, 2023).

- On average, knowledge workers lose **23 minutes** every time they switch tasks due to distractions (University of California Irvine).

The worst part? We think we're choosing what to see. We're not. The algorithms are choosing for us.

ARE YOU BEING MANIPULATED BY THE MEDIA?

I remember Jim Jones well. In 1980 (I was six years old), the *Guyana Tragedy: The Story of Jim Jones* ran as a miniseries on CBS. My parents let me watch it, mostly because my mom was super interested in what happened to Jones and his followers.

I still remember parts of it today. The drinking of the Flavor Aid (like Kool-Aid) as they committed mass suicide. Keeping the followers closed off to all outside information. Using fear as a tool to keep people obedient, scared, and paralyzed to do anything about it.

In one of the last scenes, several followers tried to escape. But others, **knowing they were going to their deaths**, drank the Flavor Aid anyway. That was the part I couldn't believe as a child.

But today it's easy to see how this can happen.

First, Jones isolated his followers in Guyana, cutting them off from outside media and communication.

Second, Jones repeated the same messages over and over again. The constant reinforcement made it difficult for his followers to think critically.

Sound familiar?

Many people we know and love have been, and are being, manipulated by the media. I know it's happened to me before.

The problem is that most people don't know they're being manipulated.

Let's do a health check on this. If you think this might be you, or perhaps one of your loved ones, ask these questions:

1. **Do you feel constantly angry or afraid?** Media manipulation triggers strong emotions, especially fear, outrage, and tribal loyalty. If everything you read or watch makes you feel like the "other side" is evil or inhuman, you might be caught in a manipulation loop.

2. **Do you only trust one side?** This is my litmus test. Recently I asked my friend: "Is there anything your party is doing that you disagree or have problems with?" If they say nothing or can't answer, they are definitely being manipulated.

3. **Do you dismiss facts you don't like?** Are you rejecting something because it's wrong or because it challenges your beliefs?

4. **Do you know the other side's argument?** Can you explain the other side's view in a way they would agree with? (That they are crazy does not count.)

5. **Have you stopped thinking for yourself?** Do you listen to your chosen media channel and de facto adopt the stance, or are you processing the information?

If you watch and listen to the same messaging over and over, day after day, odds are you are actively being manipulated. That means having any kind of rational thought over an issue is literally impossible.

Ask yourself if a source is trying to make you feel rather than help you think. If it's feel, be skeptical. If you watch the news on cable, most of the programming is opinion. You need to be aware of that.

Let's take Ryan Holiday's advice:

"Two thousand years ago, Marcus Aurelius wrote in his Meditations, 'Are you distracted by breaking news? Then take some leisure time to learn something good and stop bouncing around.'"

To follow Marcus's example then, I say: *Watch less news. Read more books.*

Jones's followers were manipulated because they were getting one source of information consistently over time. As critically thinking humans, we can't let that happen.

CURATING A FREEDOM-FRIENDLY FEED

You don't need to go off-grid. You just need to be **intentional**.

Here's how to build a mental environment that supports your clarity, energy, and creative momentum:

1. **Audit what you consume.** Go through every social app, podcast, newsletter, and media source. Ask:

   - Does this make me smarter, calmer, or more focused?

   - Or is it just giving me a dopamine hit and a distraction?

2. **Set guardrails.**

   - Delete apps off your phone (you can still use them on desktop).

   - Block distracting websites during work blocks (use tools like Freedom or Cold Turkey).

   - Use email filters to route newsletters to a dedicated "read later" folder.

3. **Be a creator first, consumer second.** Before you check social or email in the morning, **create something first**. One sentence. One idea. One email draft. Protect your direction before the world floods in.

The majority of people in the world don't audit their consumption behavior. That's a tragedy. You can't afford not to know what's feeding into your system.

CAL NEWPORT AND THE DEEP LIFE

Author and computer science professor Cal Newport doesn't use social media at all. He writes books, publishes a newsletter, teaches, and runs a podcast. That's it. His core philosophy?

"The ability to perform deep work is becoming increasingly rare at exactly the same time it is becoming increasingly valuable."

Cal believes that mental clarity is a **strategic advantage**. That your ability to think clearly, without interruption, is what separates creators from noise merchants.

You don't have to quit the internet. But you should absolutely **protect your brain like it's a business asset**.

Because it is.

TRACK YOUR TIME

Most people today feel overwhelmed in our chaotic world. They are having a hard time grasping meaning with so much going on around them.

One of my friends wanted to start a business his entire life. Let's call him Bob (not his real name). He's been talking about a particular business idea for over 20 years. Every time Bob brings it up, I tell him he should do it. Every time Bob responds that he can't. The kids this. Or the family that. Or the bills this. Or his current job that.

Listening to Bob talk is an experiment in itself. Here is Bob in a nutshell:

- He's always busy (and will tell you so).

- He doesn't know how he can get everything done in the allotted time.

- He feels he "has" to do things that he doesn't want to do.

- He makes excuses.

It's difficult for me to watch. Bob has so much talent. I want to take him and fix him. I've tried to say things here or there, but he doesn't take advice well. Simply put, all of Bob's issues are self-inflicted, and only Bob can do something about this.

If Bob were open to it, this would be my plan:

TAKE A WEEK AND TRACK YOUR TIME

Bob complains that he's always busy. I know for sure that this is his mindset and he's not actually that busy.

To fix this, I would track what he does for a full week, 24 hours a day: How much does Bob sleep? How much time does Bob spend on email? How much television does Bob watch? How much time does Bob spend scrolling through social media?

Without even trying I could find Bob an extra four to six hours a day in time (just by removing the TV and social media scrolling).

ANALYZE AND CHOOSE

Like Bob, so many people I know feel they "have to" do certain things. This is usually not true. We either make the choice consciously or make the choice by just letting it happen.

Once the list is complete, we need to create what an average day looks like. It might be easier for you to just look at a workday and leave the weekends alone.

It might look like this:

- Sleep: 7 hours

- Getting ready for work: 1 hour

- Commuting to and from work: 1 hour

- Work: 7 hours

- Breaks and lunch at work: 1 hour

- Time on phone/social media/personal email: 3 hours

- Making/having dinner: 1 hour

- Watching Netflix or TV: 3 hours

You get the point.

Now rate each one with (a) Must do, (b) Probably must do, or (c) Don't need.

In the above example, I can identify six hours right away that Bob doesn't need.

Those six hours per day, five days a week, add up to over 1,500 hours in a year. You can accomplish a lot with that kind of time. This could be the time Bob needs to start his business. Or maybe he can work to have a better relationship with his wife and kids.

The point is, Bob has the power to change his life. He just doesn't realize it.

THE 30-DAY FEED DETOX CHALLENGE

Try this for the next 30 days:

- Turn off all notifications except for calendar and calls.

- Don't check your phone for the first hour after waking.

- Subscribe to one high-quality newsletter or podcast that *challenges your thinking.*

- Set a daily media consumption limit (and stick to it).

You'll be shocked at how much time, space, and clarity you reclaim.

JOHN CLEESE AND CREATIVITY

Toward the middle of John Cleese's book *Creativity*, he talks about the greatest creativity killer.

Can you guess what it is?

It's interruption.

He says research has shown that after an interruption it can take eight minutes for you to return to your previous state of consciousness. And up to 20 minutes to get back into a state of deep focus.

Let's think about what you're creating. You start on that article or post or image or storyboard, and then someone walks outside your door. You stop. It distracted you.

You were in the groove, and now it will take you 10 minutes or more to get it back.

How about checking social media? I know a few people that keep their social media notifications on all day. Probably five minutes do not go by that they don't receive some kind of news or social update. It's a problem.

Cleese recommends two different strategies to remove these types of interruptions.

First, create boundaries of space to stop others from interrupting you. Shut the door, put "Do not disturb" on the outside, or hide where people can't bother you. Second, create boundaries of time by arranging for a specific period to preserve your boundaries of space.

For creators, this means effectively using your calendar. To finish my first novel, I blocked out calendar time every morning for my writing. It was just my computer and me locked away in my office. I left my phone outside the room.

At first this was extremely difficult. I'd interrupt myself all the time. I'd think about whom I needed to call or email, or sometimes just crazy random thoughts popped inside my brain.

But your mind learns and, after a few days, I found the groove. Those two-hour periods seemed to last just a few minutes and then . . . poof . . . I wrote 2,000 words.

Do you want to be more creative? Give yourself the time and space to do so.

As Cleese says, creativity doesn't just happen. You must protect your feed so you give creativity the opportunity to appear.

LET'S GO!

The quality of your input determines the quality of your output.

You are what you consume. So protect your feed. Guard your mind. And create from a place of clarity, not chaos.

Burn the playbook that says more information is always better. Build a mental environment that fuels your mission. You control the feed, or the feed controls you.

CHAPTER 13

STAY HEALTHY TO STAY FREE

(Why creator health is the real wealth.)

WHAT HILL SAID/WHAT IT MEANS NOW

WHAT HILL SAID (1937):

> *"Sound health begins with a sound health consciousness,
> just as financial success begins with a prosperity consciousness."*

WHAT IT MEANS NOW:

If you want to grow long term . . . creatively, financially, or personally . . . you can't neglect the vessel carrying your ambition. Health isn't a side hustle. It's the foundation of everything else.

You can't build anything meaningful if your body and brain are breaking down.

That's the hard truth most entrepreneurs ignore.

We focus on growth, revenue, audience, momentum. But the most important platform you'll ever build is the one you live inside every day: **your body**.

If you want to stay sharp, stay creative, and stay free for the long haul, you have to treat your health as your **nonnegotiable operating system**.

OBSESSION OR OPTIMIZATION?

I'm obsessive about anything I choose to do. I can't do anything halfway. Either I go overboard or I do nothing.

For the most part, that has served me well. It helped me start and sell multiple businesses, run a marathon, and stay happily married to the love of my life.

My most recent obsession? **Brain health and longevity**. Alzheimer's runs on my father's side of the family. I have friends who are suffering from it. I've seen what it can do.

That led me to *The End of Alzheimer's* by Dr. Dale Bredesen, a book that changed my view of what's possible. Not only does Bredesen claim that we can prevent cognitive decline; we can, in some cases, **reverse it**. Then I read *Outlive* by Peter Attia. And then *Super Agers* by Eric Topol.

Not everything in these books is practical for some people, and some of the data is questionable, but it gave me a direction: Optimize what I can now and build habits that compound over decades.

THREE BIG AREAS

The above three resources mimic themselves in the three areas that can help repair your body and keep it healthy.

1. CUT THE SUGAR

Two hundred years ago, we consumed around 20 grams of sugar a day. Today? Over 200 grams.

Sugar isn't just bad for your body. It's bad for your brain. It creates inflammation, insulin spikes, and long-term cognitive stress.

If you cut sugar out of your life, you'll have more control over your weight and your blood sugar, you'll have better skin, and you'll decrease the risk of almost every major disease. Enough said.

2. FAST TO RESET

Some people fast every day. This is called "intermittent fasting" (also called "time-based eating"), where a person eats inside a time window (from noon to 8 p.m., for example, known as 16:8). Other people fast 20–24 hours for one period during the week or eat one meal a day (OMAD). While there is no right way, more and more evidence shows that fasting heals the body.

It's not about deprivation. It's about giving your body time to **clean up damaged cells** via a process called "autophagy". If done right, this can create more mental focus and better long-term health for your brain.

3. DITCH THE BOXES

Bredesen has a simple rule: "If it comes in a box and has more than five ingredients, don't eat it."

The more whole foods we eat (eggs, fish, meat, fruits, vegetables), the better we feel. It's not perfect, but it's sustainable.

Please note: Some of this advice might not suit you if you are in a unique position (for example, pregnancy or significantly declining health). Please consult a doctor before you make any significant changes.

WHY THIS MATTERS FOR CREATORS

If you want to create, speak, lead, and build for the next 10, 20, 30 years, you can't ignore your foundation.

You can't out-hustle chronic fatigue. You can't build a legacy from a hospital bed.

This is the long game, and you have to **build a body and brain that can carry the weight of your dreams**.

TRAINING YOUR BRAIN

As we've discussed, neuroplasticity is the brain's ability to reorganize itself by forming new neural connections. Unfortunately, neuroplasticity doesn't just happen.

The brain won't grow if you don't stretch and work it.

Think about running a marathon. It's not possible without months and months of short runs to give you the ability to do a longer run. Or lifting weights. You have to start with a small weight and continually grow muscles over time.

The brain works the same way.

This means you must continually do things differently. Even small things.

For example, what is your dominant hand for brushing your teeth? For most people it's the right hand. So every other day, use your left hand. Do that, and the brain will start firing in completely different ways.

Here are some other examples:

- Start doing yoga.
- Journal your thoughts.
- Read books on subjects outside of what you do for a living.

There are all sorts of benefits to this, including an increase in dopamine levels and the ability to be more creative, **but the number one reason to do this is to reduce cognitive decline.**

NAVAL'S LAW OF LEVERAGE: START WITH THE BODY

In the world of tech investing, Naval Ravikant is known as a philosopher with a billionaire's wisdom. He cofounded AngelList, backed dozens of start-ups, and wrote viral Twitter/X threads that became scripture for some digital entrepreneurs.

But the secret to his success didn't come from code or capital . . . it started with health.

After years of chasing financial wins, Naval found himself exhausted and mentally foggy. No amount of success could override the stress creeping into his system. That's when he made a radical shift.

"I realized my body was my real leverage," he says. "If you're sick or tired, it doesn't matter how many opportunities come your way . . . you won't have the energy to seize them."

So Naval rewired his habits.

He started strength training regularly. He walked in the sun every day. He fasted, eliminated processed foods, and prioritized eight hours of sleep. And, most importantly, he became obsessive about reading, meditating, and removing clutter from his mind.

The impact?

He didn't just *feel* better. His thinking became clearer. His decisions sharper. His relationships deeper. "A fit body and a calm mind," he says, "is how you create wealth, not the other way around."

Naval isn't a monk or a bodybuilder. He's a pragmatist. And he reminds us of the most overlooked truth in creator life:

"If your health goes, everything else becomes optional. If your health holds, everything else becomes possible."

LONGEVITY CHECKLIST—THE DAILY PLAN FOR STAYING SHARP AND FREE

If you want to create for the long haul and stay clear, focused, and energetic while doing it, you need a daily rhythm that supports both your body and your brain.

Based on research from Dr. Dale Bredesen, from Dr. Peter Attia, and from what's working in my own life, here's a simple, sustainable plan to start with:

Daily Movement

- Aim for 30–45 minutes of moderate-intensity exercise.
- Combine **aerobic** (walking, running, cycling) with **resistance training** (bodyweight exercises, bands, or weights).

"Muscle mass is one of the most important predictors of longevity."

—Dr. Peter Attia

Time-Restricted Eating

- Eat during an 8–10-hour window (e.g., 11 a.m.–7 p.m.).
- Fast for 12–16 hours overnight to promote autophagy (cell repair).

Note: Some people don't cope well with time-restricted eating, so if it doesn't work for you, just follow the rest.

Real Food Only

- Focus on whole, unprocessed foods: eggs, fish, meat, vegetables, berries, nuts.
- Reduce or eliminate sugar, processed carbs, seed oils.

Sleep Like It's Your Job

- Get seven to eight hours per night.
- Prioritize **deep sleep** and track it if needed (Oura, WHOOP, Apple Watch).

Nutrient Support

- Consider taking a multivitamin, omega-3s, and vitamin D.
- Test for hormone/nutrient deficiencies yearly and address gaps.

Mental Fitness

- Read, learn, write, problem solve.
- Stay curious. Avoid making judgments and, instead, try to understand why people do or believe something.

"Cognitive decline is not inevitable if we train the brain like we train the body."

—Dr. Peter Attia

Stress Management

- Daily practices: breathing, prayer, meditation, or gratitude.
- Less screen time. More quiet time.

WHAT IS AUTOPHAGY?

Autophagy (from the Greek for "self-eating") is your body's natural cellular recycling system. When triggered, especially during fasting, your cells break down and remove damaged parts, turning biological clutter into clean energy.

In 2016, Japanese scientist **Dr. Yoshinori Ohsumi** won the Nobel Prize in Physiology or Medicine for uncovering how autophagy works.

His research linked the process to improved immune function, reduced inflammation, and increased longevity.

Translation: Give your body a break from constant eating, and it gets to work *repairing you.*

Longevity is not luck. It's the accumulation of thousands of small, intentional choices.

You don't need to be perfect. You just need to start and stay consistent.

If you want to grow old and make an impact on the world, you need to stay healthy.

And you need two longevity plans:

1. **A health plan**
2. **A purpose plan** (most of this book)

One keeps your body alive. The other keeps your spirit lit.

LET'S GO!

You don't need six-pack abs or biohacker gear. You need a simple, sustainable system that keeps you **sharp, focused, and consistent.**

Burn the playbook that glorifies burnout. Stay healthy to stay free, and give your future self a chance to thrive.

CHAPTER 14

UPGRADE YOUR MENTAL OPERATING SYSTEM

(A strong mind builds a strong future.)

WHAT HILL SAID/WHAT IT MEANS NOW

WHAT HILL SAID (1937):

"Whatever the mind can conceive and believe, it can achieve."

WHAT IT MEANS NOW:

Your identity isn't fixed. Your mindset is malleable. You can rewrite your beliefs, rewire your patterns, and reinvent your future.

Most people never question the software running their lives. They run the same routines, chase the same validation, and operate with the same mental scripts they absorbed unconsciously as kids, students, or employees.

They stay stuck; not because they lack talent, but because **their thinking hasn't been updated in decades.**

If you want to be free, not just financially but emotionally and mentally, you need to **upgrade your operating system.**

This chapter is about rethinking how you think.

WHY MOST PEOPLE NEVER CHANGE

Change is hard. Not because new habits are difficult but because **old stories are powerful.**

We believe:

- "I'm just not disciplined."
- "I'm not creative."
- "I've never been good with money."
- "I need permission to try something new."

These stories aren't facts. They're *scripts*. And most of them were written by someone else.

Until you rewrite the code, you'll keep living by default, not design.

WHAT THE DATA SAYS

- According to Stanford psychologist Carol Dweck, people with a **growth mindset** (those who believe they can develop skills through effort) outperform those with a fixed mindset across almost every domain.
- Behavioral scientist BJ Fogg found that **tiny habit changes,** anchored to existing routines, are far more effective than motivation-based plans.

- Your beliefs literally reshape your brain. Repeated thoughts form new neural pathways. This is the science of **neuroplasticity**.

Your brain is plastic. It's bendable. The question is, **what are you programming into it daily?**

THE SABBATICAL THAT REBOOTED MY MIND

After selling my company in 2016, I spent 2018 on a full sabbatical.

No business travel. No content marketing. No social media. No inbox.

I went electronics-free for 30 days. I read actual books. Made daily lunches for my kids. Repaired the backyard lights (twice). Finished writing a novel. Ran personal bests in the half marathon and 10K. Spent time with my kids at night.

The biggest shift? I stopped measuring my time by output and started noticing the people around me again.

I didn't miss the news. I missed nothing from the industry. But I noticed everything:

- How much I'd been addicted to checking email and the stock market
- How much noise was clogging my thinking
- How just being present was 90 percent of parenting

The sabbatical didn't make me less productive. It made me more human.

If your brain is overloaded, your calendar a mess, and you can't remember the last time you felt **quiet,** consider a reset. Not to stop the work. But to return stronger, lighter, and clearer about what actually matters.

The good news? You don't need 12 months to make this happen. You can do it in a month, a week, or even a weekend.

REPROGRAM YOUR INPUTS

If you want to upgrade your output, start by upgrading what you feed your mind:

- **Read great books** (not just business, but philosophy, psychology, biography).
- **Follow fewer people, more closely**. Quality over volume.
- **Journal every morning** (even three minutes can clarify your thinking).
- **Limit exposure to chaos** (politics and gossip).
- **Do things that slow you down**. Puzzles, cooking, long walks, real conversations.

Mental strength isn't loud. It's quiet. But it's what allows everything else to hold up under pressure.

YOU ARE WHAT YOU THINK ABOUT

Jay Shetty built his incredible media empire on the idea of mindfulness and purpose. He often says, "You are what you think about."

For example, if you go to sleep saying you are tired, your mind will process that during the night, and you'll feel (or think you are) tired in the morning. That will continue throughout the day, and the cycle will continue.

But if you say you are going to have a very productive day tomorrow, you will wake up feeling productive and more likely to do things that are productive.

Shetty says the best thing to do is to write down your intentions for the next day and review them before you go to sleep.

The brain is bendable.

DESIGN A BETTER INTERNAL SCRIPT

Your identity is not a fixed thing. It's a **story in progress.**

Here's how to start rewriting it:

1. **Identify your default script.**

- "I'm bad at X."

- "I always quit."

- "I'm just not wired that way."

2. **Replace it with a chosen script:**

- "I'm becoming someone who completes projects every week."

- "I follow through even when it's difficult."

- "I protect my time because I know where I'm going."

3. **Anchor it to action.** Every time you repeat a new habit, you cast a vote for your new identity. As James Clear says, **"You become your habits."**

THE "CAN'T" JAR

When Jessica Lahey, educator and author of *The Gift of Failure*, noticed her students (and her own children) constantly saying, "I can't," she realized it wasn't about ability. It was about mindset.

So she started a family experiment.

She placed a large, empty glass jar on the kitchen counter and labeled it **"The Can't Jar."** Every time someone in the house said, "I can't do this," "I'll never figure it out," or "I'm just not good at this," they had to drop a coin into the jar.

Then came the follow-up: They had to reframe the sentence out loud.

"I can't do this" became "I haven't figured this out *yet*."

"I'm just not good at math" turned into "I'm learning how to get better at math."

It started as a joke. But quickly, it changed the language inside their house.

The jar filled slowly. Then not at all.

Because the real shift wasn't about quarters. It was about rewiring the brain to see challenges as opportunities. Failure as feedback. Effort as a path forward.

This is mental software in action. You don't need to overhaul your life. You just need to upgrade your default responses.

LET'S GO!

Your body is your hardware. Your brain is your operating system. And your beliefs are the code.

If you want to live free, think clearly, and create boldly, you have to rewrite the script you've been running for too long.

Burn the playbook that says your mindset is fixed. Upgrade your mental OS and watch what happens next.

CHAPTER 15

LISTEN TO THE WHISPER

(The signal is quiet. Are you paying attention?)

WHAT HILL SAID/WHAT IT MEANS NOW

WHAT HILL SAID (1937):

"The sixth sense is that portion of the subconscious mind which has been referred to as the Creative Imagination."

WHAT IT MEANS NOW:

You don't need more data. You need more stillness. That's when your deeper self speaks. If you're listening, you'll know what to do next.

✖✖✖

Most of the time, the world screams: Notifications. Algorithms. Headlines. Urgencies.

Everything is loud. Everything is now.

But purpose? Purpose whispers.

That next big decision you're unsure about. The creative idea you keep pushing away. The thing you think you're not ready for. The version of yourself you secretly want to become . . .

Those don't show up in bold font. They show up as a nudge. A gut feeling. A recurring thought. A quiet pull toward something deeper.

Most people miss it. Not because it's unclear. But because they're never quiet enough to hear it.

JR Lay, author of the book *Banking on Change*, describes it this way:

"I can 100% recommend to others to listen to the whisper sooner than later. The more you wait to respond to the whisper, the louder it becomes. Like the roar of a lion. You can't hide from it. You can't push it away. You can't fight it.

Courage is not the absence of fear but doing what the whisper calls you to do in the face of fear . . . even when the path is not 100% clear."

WHY THE WHISPER MATTERS

The whisper isn't just your intuition. It's your **inner guidance system**.

It's the reason you feel restless after too many weeks doing something safe. It's the voice that tells you, "This isn't it," even when things are technically working. It's the recurring idea that won't leave you alone.

Ignore it long enough, and it becomes frustration. Listen to it early enough, and it becomes a calling.

WHAT THE DATA SAYS

- A study from *Harvard Business Review* found that entrepreneurs who regularly make time for **unstructured thinking** are **more creative, less reactive, and more decisive** under pressure.

- In neuroscience, this kind of space is called **default mode network activation**. This is the state your brain enters when you're doing nothing and your subconscious begins sorting the real work.

Creative breakthroughs rarely happen during planning. They happen in the gaps: **in the shower, on a walk, or during silence.**

CASE STUDY: THE IDEA I ALMOST IGNORED

The idea for *Content Inc.* came to me not at my desk, not in a brainstorm, but in the in-between.

It was a pattern I started noticing during a quiet stretch. I wasn't actively hunting for a business model. I was thinking, walking, reflecting.

The whisper was:

"The most successful businesses I'm seeing began with building an audience and then launched a product."

It seemed too simple. Too obvious. But it wouldn't leave.

Eventually, I followed it. I began writing what became the *Content Inc.* book in 2013, finished in 2014 and republished in 2021. If not for that book, *Burn the Playbook* wouldn't exist.

Thankfully that model (build audience, then product) has helped people all over the world find their own version of financial freedom.

HOW TO CREATE SPACE TO HEAR IT

You don't *need* to go off-grid. You just need a bit of *margin*.

Here's how to make room for the whisper:

- Walk without headphones.
- Watch where your mind drifts when you're bored.
- Notice the thoughts that show up more than once.

Clarity doesn't come from cramming more in.

It comes from carving space *out*.

STEPHEN KING AND THE WHISPER THAT ALMOST GOT TOSSED

Stephen King was teaching high school English and living in a trailer when he wrote the first few pages of *Carrie*. It was about a teenage girl with telekinetic powers and a brutal high school life. After a few pages, he hated it. Thought it was garbage. He crumpled it up and threw it in the trash.

His wife, Tabitha, found the pages in the bin, read them, and told him to keep going. "*This is good*," she said. "*You need to finish it*."

He listened.

King finished *Carrie*, and it became his first published novel and his first bestseller. The paperback rights alone earned him $400,000 (in 1970s money). It was the whisper that opened the door to everything else.

Even today, King says he doesn't outline heavily. He starts with a situation, a spark, a gut pull, and then listens. He follows the characters. He trusts the whisper.

THE IOWA GAMBLING TASK

In the 1990s, neuroscientist António Damásio conducted a now-famous study at the University of Iowa called the "Iowa Gambling Task." The study aimed to explore how people make decisions. It uncovered something incredible about intuition.

Participants played a card game involving four decks. Two decks offered high rewards but also massive penalties. The other two offered smaller, consistent rewards . . . and were safer in the long run.

Here's the kicker: **Long before participants could consciously explain which decks were risky, their bodies already knew.**

Electrodermal sensors showed that their palms began to sweat, indicating stress, whenever they reached for the risky decks.

That's intuition. That's the whisper.

The body was sounding an alarm before the conscious brain caught up.

Damásio called this the **somatic marker hypothesis,** the idea that our brains store emotional signals as shortcuts for decision-making. These markers surface as hunches, gut feelings, or subtle hesitations.

In short, **the whisper isn't random**. It's memory and experience speaking to you through the body, before the rational brain can explain it.

LET'S GO!

Your deepest truth isn't buried in the chaos. It's waiting in the quiet.

Make time for the silence. Follow the recurring nudges. And when the whisper shows up again, *don't ignore it this time.*

Burn the playbook that says hustle brings answers. The whisper already knows. All you have to do is listen.

CHAPTER 16

BUILD THE SYSTEM THAT FREES YOU

(Freedom is not the absence of structure. It's the result of the right one.)

WHAT HILL SAID/WHAT IT MEANS NOW

WHAT HILL SAID (1937):

*"Success requires no apologies. Failure permits no alibis.
If you are not succeeding, examine the system under which you
are operating."*

WHAT IT MEANS NOW:

Don't blame your ambition. Don't blame your goals. If something's
breaking, fix the system it lives inside.

Most people think freedom means *no rules*. No boss. No schedule. No responsibilities.

But here's the paradox: The most *truly* free people I know have more structure in their lives, not less.

They wake up with purpose. They know what matters each day. They're not in a constant spin, trying to remember who they are or what they said yes to.

Freedom isn't chaos. **It's clarity with boundaries**.

If you want to live a creative life on your terms, you need a system.

"I'm getting better every day for the rest of my life."

—Jeremy Renner

CHAOS IS EXPENSIVE

When you don't have a system, everything costs more:

- Mental bandwidth
- Emotional energy
- Time lost to indecision
- Momentum lost to distraction
- Money lost to inefficiency

Even small decisions about what to eat, when to write, and where to post add up and drain your capacity to focus on the work that matters most.

Why did Steve Jobs wear the same clothes every day? So he could free up the mental energy he'd have spent deciding what to wear and use it for something more important (like revolutionizing how we communicate with each other).

You don't rise to the level of your goals. You fall to the level of your systems.

WHAT THE DATA SAYS

- According to *Atomic Habits* author James Clear, habits save us from "decision fatigue" by automating small choices and freeing our minds for higher-level thinking.

- The most successful entrepreneurs tend to run their days with some form of structured routine . . . even if they work for themselves.

- Research from the University of Southern California found that **routines reduce anxiety and increase long-term goal attainment,** not because they're strict, but because they provide scaffolding for the creative brain.

THE PERSONAL OPERATING SYSTEM

Here's the truth: I'm not naturally disciplined.

I can be obsessive. I can work hard. But what keeps me consistent are the **systems** I've built around how I show up daily, weekly, and monthly.

Here's a version of what that looks like for me:

Daily

- Wake up and journal.
- Read 10 pages.
- Exercise (run or strength).
- Write or create first; consume later.
- Eat within an eight hour window
- Sleep seven to eight hours

Weekly

- Record podcast (2).

- Review goals.

- Block two to three focused creative hours.

- Take a walk without input.

- Dedicate one hour for relationship check-ins (home and work).

Monthly

- Review financials (personal + business).

- Revisit goals + habits.

- Block one full day off-grid.

- Check for "clutter creep" (digital, commitments, mental).

- Reorganize my desk.

This isn't rigid. It's a flexible structure.

The point is to **build something that protects your freedom** so you don't get swept away by everyone else's priorities.

BUILD YOUR OWN

Want a starting point? Start simple:

1. **Pick one daily nonnegotiable.**

- Meditate. Journal. Walk. One thing you own every day.

2. **Design a "deep work" block.**

- 90 minutes. No phone. One goal. One outcome.

3. **Set weekly rituals.**

- Review wins. Set your one big goal. Schedule it.

4. **Automate your off-time.**

- Don't check email after 6 p.m.

- Take one screen-free day per week.
- Plan fun like you plan work.

AI IS NOT THE ANSWER. IT'S THE AMPLIFIER

AI won't save your business. But it can *speed it up and scale it.*

The AI hype is real, but so is the confusion. Too many creators think ChatGPT or Google Genesis *is* the work. It's not. These tools are accelerators. They remove friction. They give you leverage.

But they can't replace:

- Your **Tilt**
- Your **voice**
- Your **values**
- Your **desire to serve a real audience**

Here's how to think about it:

Bad idea + AI = faster garbage

Clear Tilt + AI = exponential growth

Do not use AI to replace your instincts, voice, or purpose. That's how you end up with generic content that earns no trust and no revenue.

AI is not a shortcut to mattering. But it's an incredible tool once you figure out what really matters.

HOW TO ACTUALLY USE AI IN YOUR CONTENT BUSINESS

Here's how to use AI *without losing your edge*:

1. **Brainstorm faster.** Use tools like ChatGPT or Claude to generate:

- Headline variations

- Episode titles

- Outline ideas

- Naming options for your offer or newsletter

Prompt tip: "Give me 10 unconventional podcast titles about [your topic] with a curious, punchy tone."

2. **Repurpose efficiently.** You don't need to rewrite everything from scratch. Use AI to:

- Turn a podcast transcript into a blog post.

- Turn a blog post into 10 YouTube short ideas.

- Summarize long-form content for LinkedIn or a newsletter.

Tools: I use Descript for my *Content Inc.* podcast.

3. **Research and summarize.** AI can speed up your market research. Ask:

- "What are the top five challenges small-town entrepreneurs face today?"

- "Summarize this article in five bullet points I can share in my newsletter."

It's almost always *not* 100 percent accurate, so verify the results.

Since ChatGPT released its "deep research" function, I've worked with the tool to develop a number of in-depth research pieces, including the initial research for the chapter in this book on underserved audiences.

4. **Use system support (your invisible assistant).** Let AI handle the admin:

- To create content calendars

- To rewrite LinkedIn bios

- To proofread
- To generate SOPs or onboarding docs

This is where you start reclaiming time without hiring a full team.

FINAL THOUGHT

AI doesn't remove the need for trust. It doesn't replace consistency, service, or originality.

And as Simon Sinek says, your AI journey is the most important, not the output. Anyone with AI can create the output, but what you put into make the "thing" is what separates the winners and losers. Think of AI more as a coach and not your writer or outsourced creator.

But if you've got a Tilt and a vision, AI gives you a creative exoskeleton. More reach. More reps. Less drag.

Be careful. AI can, and probably will detract from your own creative journey if you let it.

I've found much of the writing and content creation process occurs in the *in between*: The thinking of topics. The consternation over using the proper word. When your brain unveils a connection you didn't think was there. All these things get the brain of a writer firing in all kinds of directions.

So when a writer leverages AI to offload many of these "chores" sometimes the writing falls flat. But even worse, the next time we begin the writing process we'll need that AI crutch again. After all this, what does writing become?

Use your best judgement and don't lose yourself in the process.

AI MIGHT NOT BE ENOUGH

AI will only be able to get you so far. That's when it's time to bring in help, but without building the very thing you escaped: a job you hate or a business that owns you.

After considering leveraging AI tools, here's how to scale smart:

- **Start with contractors**. Look for virtual assistants (VAs), writers, editors, designers, or customer service freelancers. Start part-time. Use clear SOPs. Keep control of your voice and vision.

- **Use fractional pros**. Need CFO-level insight, legal review, or a marketing strategist? Fractional executives give you high-level talent without full-time costs.

- **Test with projects**. Start with a small, low-stakes task. If it works, scale it. If it doesn't, move on. No harm, no contract.

- **Watch for "management creep."** If you're spending more time managing than creating, you've gone too far. Your goal is leverage, not layers.

Rule of thumb: Only hire when it gives you *more focus, not less*.

My wife and I built Content Marketing Institute into a $10 million business. We did this with only two full-time employees: the two of us. To help us, we built an amazing team of 28 contractors.

We found these people in several ways. We found our lead editor, Michele Linn, after following her on Twitter/X. I met our lead strategist, Robert Rose, at a speaking event. Peter Loibl, our head of sales, was an intern at an association I belonged to. Laura Kozak, our web operations lead, and JK Kalinowski, our creative director, were both a part of our local early-childhood PTA. Cathy McPhillips, who became our head of marketing, was a friend of someone we went to church with.

Observation creates opportunity. So, wherever you are, be present and pay attention, and it will pay off.

JACK BUTCHER—ONE SYSTEM, GLOBAL IMPACT

Jack Butcher, the designer behind *Visualize Value*, didn't build a business by grinding 16 hours a day.

He built a repeatable system:

- One image. One idea. Every day.
- Simple, black-and-white visuals that communicate clarity.

He posted daily on Twitter/X and Instagram. He packaged his frameworks into digital products. He built a self-serve system for buyers.

The result? A multimillion-dollar brand, 400,000+ followers, and a growing vault of timeless products. All while keeping his work simple, repeatable, and aligned.

Jack's structure *created* his freedom.

LEGO AND THE PARADOX OF CREATIVE FREEDOM

If you give a kid a blank canvas or paper and say, "Make anything," they usually freeze. But hand them a box of LEGO bricks with a few clear constraints using colors, shapes, or a build guide, and they're off to the races. Why?

Because **structure gives freedom boundaries to push against.**

LEGO mastered this. Its system is built on uniformity: Every brick, no matter when or where it was made, snaps together with every other piece. This constraint is what makes limitless creativity possible. The *structure* is what unlocks the play.

Now imagine if every LEGO brick was a different size or shape. Chaos. Creativity would stall. Progress would slow. Nothing would fit.

The same is true in your business and life. When you build a simple, repeatable system . . . your own creative LEGO set . . . you remove the friction. You free up your energy for deep work, great ideas, and momentum.

LET'S GO!

Stop trying to wing it. Stop reacting to every shiny opportunity.

Build a structure that protects your energy, focuses your attention, and reinforces who you're becoming.

Burn the playbook that says freedom is accidental. The most liberated people you know? They have a system. Now it's your turn.

CHAPTER 17

MAKING THE LEAP

(How to go from paycheck prisoner to self-directed freedom builder.)

WHAT HILL SAID/WHAT IT MEANS NOW

WHAT HILL SAID (1937):

"Do not wait. The time will never be just right."

WHAT IT MEANS NOW:

There will never be a perfect financial moment. Never a clear signal from the universe. Never full certainty. You make the leap *before* you feel ready. Then build the muscle while falling.

So you're stuck. You feel like your job is sucking the life out of you. And if you have a "side hustle," or the thing you *actually* care about, it is barely hanging on by threads of time, energy, and belief.

Welcome to the tension. This chapter is your map out of it.

THE PARABLE OF THE LOCKED BOX

There was once a person who spent their whole life staring at a locked box on their desk.

They received the box as a young adult the day they took their first corporate job. It came with a note:

"Inside this box is everything you truly want. But once opened, you cannot go back."

At first, they were curious. What could be inside? A dream business? A book unwritten? A calling?

But then came the meetings. The promotions. The mortgage. The comfort of routine.

They said to themselves, "I'll open it next year. When things are calmer. When I've saved a bit more."

Decades passed. They kept the box polished but untouched. They even warned others, "Be careful with that kind of thing. You can lose everything."

On the day of their retirement, they finally opened the box.

It was empty.

Not because there was never anything inside . . . but because the contents only appear for those willing to take the risk to look.

I HATE THE TERM "SIDE HUSTLE"

Let's call this what it is: a slow-motion identity crisis.

Most people don't start a side hustle because they want more income. They start it because they want *out*.

- The accountant who records and publishes movie reviews on TikTok
- The admin building a tiny AI course community on her lunch break

- The marketer who makes golf videos at 5 a.m. before Zoom meetings

This isn't hustling. It's gasping for air.

The real problem? We're treating our passion like a side project and our job like a prison sentence. And most people never switch them.

FLIP THE SCRIPT

Here's the shift: Make your current job the side hustle. The income engine.

Make your side hustle the main thing. The purpose engine.

You're not quitting blindly. You're reprioritizing on purpose.

Your day job becomes what funds your freedom and not what *defines* your identity.

REGRET MINIMIZATION FRAMEWORK

Jeff Bezos's **Regret Minimization Framework** is a mental model he used to guide one of the most important decisions of his life: whether to leave his secure job on Wall Street to start Amazon in 1994.

Here's how it works:

Imagine yourself at age 80. Look back on your life and ask yourself, "Will I regret not having done this?"

If the answer is yes, that regret will likely outweigh the risks or fears of doing the thing today. Bezos believed that **regret for things not done** is far more painful than regret for things that failed. He explained:

"I knew that when I was 80, I was not going to regret having tried this. I was not going to regret trying to participate in this thing called the Internet that I thought was going to be a really big deal. I knew that if I failed I wouldn't regret that, but I knew the one thing I might regret is not ever having tried. I knew that would haunt me every day."

HOW IT APPLIES TO YOUR LEAP

Use this framework when deciding to leave your job, start a business, publish your book, launch your podcast . . . whatever your version of the leap is.

Ask:

- At 80, would I regret **not trying?**
- Am I staying where I am because it's safe or because it's right?
- Will this decision age well?

It's a compass for big decisions, especially when fear clouds your vision.

DO I JUST QUIT?

Not yet. Maybe not for a while.

But you do start acting like you *will* quit soon.

You:

- Cut unnecessary expenses and map your "FU budget."
- Test your content or offer consistently.
- Build a three to six month runway of savings if possible.
- Start monetizing *something* to prove you can.
- Create a "go date" and work backward.

You're not being impulsive. You're being strategic. And honest.

HOW MUCH MONEY DO I NEED?

As much as possible.

But here's the better question: What's the minimum monthly income you can live on while building your new life?

This is your **baseline freedom number**. It's probably lower than you think.

If your job pays $80,000 but you only need $55,000 to live lean, your runway might be closer than you realize.

When I made the jump in 2007, here's what I did:

- Went from two cars to one
- Settled for local vacations with the family instead of longer, more expensive trips
- Had more home-cooked meals and ate out less
- Made a pot of coffee instead of getting Starbucks

One off, these are not big moves. But combined, it made a big deal toward a simpler lifestyle, which not only helped my wallet but increased my focus.

WILL MY FAMILY FREAK OUT?

Maybe. Probably. That's okay.

They want safety. That's their job. Your job is vision.

Have the conversation. Share the plan. Involve them where possible. But remember, they don't need to get it. They just need to respect it.

But here's the hard truth. If you have a significant other that doesn't support your efforts or believe you can make this happen, it will be incredibly difficult. This thing you are doing is already a huge challenge. Creating tension at home is not just icing on the cake . . . it's the whole thing. Knowing this up front will help you make the right decision.

CAN I PREPARE FOR EVERYTHING?

Nope.

There will be fear. Chaos. Uncertainty. Self-doubt. There will also be adrenaline, joy, and unexpected momentum.

You're not looking for comfort. You're looking for *alignment*.

There is no "right" time. There's just *your* time. And you get to choose when that starts.

WHAT TO EXPECT

Unexpected Sacrifices

- Loneliness

- Income dips

- Family doubt

- Feeling like a fraud

- Canceling Netflix (yeah, really)

Unexpected Gifts

- Time freedom

- Clarity

- Loving Mondays

- Momentum you actually earned

- Your kids seeing what's possible

THE TOP FIVE REGRETS

In her book *The Top Five Regrets of the Dying*, palliative care nurse **Bronnie Ware** collected insights from hundreds of patients in their final days. The most common regret?

"I wish I'd had the courage to live a life true to myself, not the life others expected of me."

That's it. Not more money. Not a different job title. Not even more time. **It was about never making the leap.**

Ware describes patients who stayed in jobs they hated, never pursued their passions, or ignored the whisper of a calling because it seemed too risky. They waited. And waited. Until the clock ran out.

One of her patients, a man named John, had always wanted to open a small café and write a book. He spent his life in corporate finance instead. "It was always 'next year,'" he said. "But I ran out of next years."

Regret isn't loud. It doesn't slam doors or shout in meetings. It's quiet. It sits in your chest when you're alone and wonders what could have been.

LET'S GO!

You don't have to quit tomorrow.

But you *do* have to quit lying to yourself about how long you'll wait.

Don't let the job you hate steal the life you want. Flip the script. Reclaim your path. Make the leap.

Even if it's messy. Even if it's slow. Even if no one claps.

Because the future you are building?

It's worth it.

CONCLUSION

BURN IT AND BUILD IT

(You don't need their playbook. You need your own.)

If you've made it this far, you already know the truth: You can't keep doing things the way they've always been done. Not if you want freedom. Not if you want meaning. Not if you want to matter.

The old system—go to school, get the job, climb the ladder, retire, and hope you're still healthy—isn't broken. It was never designed to work for *you* in the first place.

So now you face choices: **what to burn and what to build**.

What Will You Burn?

- Burn the timeline that says you're behind.
- Burn the corporate script that rewards silence and sameness.
- Burn the myth that more credentials mean more credibility.
- Burn the belief that success means sacrifice.
- Burn the fear of starting small.
- Burn the idea that your value depends on external approval.

The people who win today are not the loudest or the luckiest. They're the ones who are willing to let go of the system that isn't serving them and build something that does.

What Will You Build?

- Build your Tilt.
- Build the system that frees you.
- Build income streams that work while you sleep.
- Build your health so you can stay in the game.
- Build your crew: the people who'll tell you the truth and walk beside you.
- Build habits that shape the person you want to become.

And most of all, **build with purpose**.

This isn't about hacks or hustle. It's about building something that lasts.

It's about building something that reflects your values. Something you can be proud to hand down, pass on, or stand behind.

YOU ALREADY KNOW ENOUGH

Don't let the world convince you that you need to wait.

You don't need more credentials. You don't need a bigger audience. You don't need permission.

You just need the courage to trust your instincts and take the first step.

You now have a different kind of playbook. But what you do with it?

That's on you.

"There is only today, with holes in our pockets, with time spilling out. We cannot keep it for tomorrow."

—Erin Loechner

A FINAL NOTE

If you're one of the few who finishes this book and takes action, I promise you this: You will be misunderstood. You will be doubted. You will face resistance. Especially from the people who benefit from you staying stuck.

But if you stay the course, if you surround yourself with the right people, if you listen to the whisper and move before you feel ready . . .

You will change your life, and you will change the lives of others.

You will make an impact on the world and make it just a bit better.

Not overnight. But completely.

TO MY KIDS

You don't have to follow someone else's plan (especially mine). You don't have to wait to be chosen. You are allowed to want more . . . on your terms.

And when life feels loud, or heavy, or uncertain, remember this:

You are not stuck. You can burn what no longer fits. And you can build something better.

And whatever happens, you are loved.

KEEP GOING

If this book lit something in you . . . an idea, a shift, a fire . . . don't let it fade. Keep the momentum alive:

Get my free every-other-week newsletter where I share one powerful idea for creators and content entrepreneurs trying to build something they own.

→ joepulizzi.com

Whatever your next step is, take it. Your freedom lives on the other side of momentum.

And if you ever feel stuck? Flip back to Chapter 1. This time you won't be starting from scratch. You'll be starting from experience. Are you made for more? I believe you are.

NOW GO!

Don't wait. Don't settle. Don't sleepwalk through someone else's definition of success.

Burn what doesn't serve you. Build what matters.

And never look back.

"Because you might as well be dead. Seriously, if you always put limits on what you can do, physical or anything else, it'll spread over into the rest of your life. It'll spread into your work, into your morality, into your entire being. There are no limits. There are plateaus, but you must not stay there, you must go beyond them. If it kills you, it kills you. A man must constantly exceed his level."

—Bruce Lee

BUT BEFORE YOU GO: YOUR BUILD-WHAT-MATTERS CHECKLIST

(Reading is good. Doing is better.)

If there's one thing this book should leave you with, it's this: **You are not stuck. But if you want freedom, you must move.**

Below is your go-forward checklist. The things to start doing, reviewing, or shifting *right now* to build a life that's yours.

1. **Find your Tilt.**

    - List 10 things you're deeply curious about.

    - Combine ideas: Where's the unusual overlap?

    - Pick one underserved audience.

    - Be specific. Be weird. Be real.

2. **Upgrade your belief system.**

    - Write your new identity in present tense: "I am a person who follows through."

    - Journal daily (three to five minutes is enough).

    - Talk to your future self in writing.

- *Remember*: You become what you repeat.

3. Build your daily system.

- Set a creative rhythm: When do you write, record, reflect, or make?
- Protect your mornings: Create before you consume.
- Establish one daily nonnegotiable.
- Block deep-work time at least twice per week.

4. Design your FU financial plan.

- Spend less than you earn.
- Pay off all credit cards monthly.
- Open and contribute to a Roth IRA.
- Build an emergency fund.
- Add a second income stream within the next 12 months.

5. Protect your health for the long game.

- Eat more whole foods and fewer packaged ones.
- Exercise daily, even if just 10 minutes.
- Sleep seven to eight hours.
- Reduce sugar and alcohol intake.
- Keep learning (books, puzzles, challenges).

6. Control your feed.

- Turn off most notifications.
- Take one screen-free hour per day.
- Read more books than social posts.

7. Build a freedom-friendly business model.

- Create a scalable asset: book, product, membership.

- Stack revenue streams gradually.

- Focus on high-leverage activities: audience building, content, offers.

- Systematize what works (automate and delegate).

8. Curate your crew.

- Identify three to five key voices: truth-teller, peer, connector, expert, superfan.

- Join or start a mastermind.

- Be around people who remind you of who you're becoming.

9. Make room for the whisper.

- Journal in silence.

- Walk without headphones.

- Track recurring ideas (they often hold the next move).

- Don't dismiss the quiet thoughts; follow them.

10. Review and adjust monthly.

- What's working? What's noisy? What needs to go?

- Are you building freedom or just busyness?

- Revisit this list every 30 days and recommit to what matters.

START SMALL. STAY CONSISTENT

You don't have to do all of this today. But if you pick even *one thing* and do it consistently, momentum will follow.

Progress comes from clarity. Freedom comes from action.

Now . . . choose one line above. Highlight it. Bookmark it. Do it.

And begin.

WHEN IT GETS HARD

There will be days when the algorithm tanks your views, your inbox is empty, your friends question your choices, and your bank account is troubling you.

This is the part no one talks about enough.

Keep going.

Momentum is invisible until it breaks through. Most people quit at the exact moment it begins to build.

Come back to your Tilt. Go back to your reason. Then take the next small, intentional step.

The difference between those who make it and those who don't? **One more day. One more try. One more rep.**

When it gets hard, show up anyway. That's the real playbook.

BURN THE PLAYBOOK: THE 21-DAY CHALLENGE

(Build momentum. One small win at a time.)

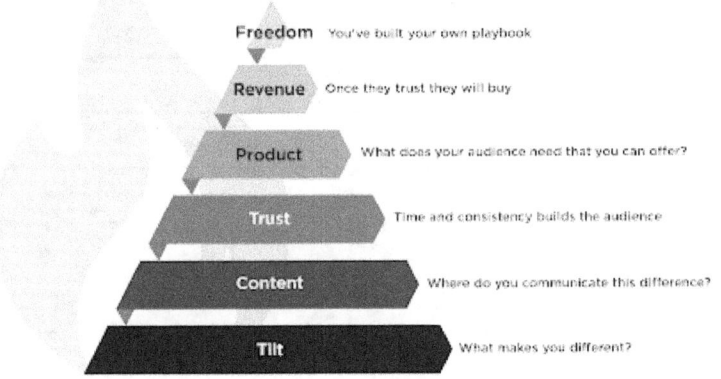

The Burn the Playbook Pyramid

Freedom — You've built your own playbook

Revenue — Once they trust they will buy

Product — What does your audience need that you can offer?

Trust — Time and consistency builds the audience

Content — Where do you communicate this difference?

Tilt — What makes you different?

Courtesy JK Kalinowski

WEEK 1: BURN THE OLD BELIEFS

Goal: Let go of outdated mindsets and get clarity on your Tilt.

DAY 1—WRITE YOUR "WHY."

Why are you here? Why did you pick up this book? Write three to five sentences on what you truly want to build.

_____

_____

_____

_____

_____

DAY 2—FIND 10 CURIOSITIES.

List 10 things you're endlessly curious about. Don't judge them. Just list them.

1. _____

2. _____

3. _____

4. _____

5. _____

6. _____

7. _____

8. _____

9. _____

10. _____

DAY 3—DEFINE YOUR TILT.

Look at your list. Which ideas combine in an unusual way? Which audience needs help with that?

Recombinations

_____

_____

_____

_____

_____

Audiences You Can Serve

_____

_____

_____

_____

_____

DAY 4—WRITE A NEW IDENTITY STATEMENT.

"I am someone who _____."

(*Example*: "shows up consistently" or "owns my time.")

_____

_____

_____

_____

DAY 5—DO A TIME AUDIT.

Track everything you do today. Where are you leaking energy?

_____

_____

_____

_____

_____

DAY 6—DELETE THREE DISTRACTIONS.

Unsubscribe from a newsletter. Turn off notifications. Remove a social app.

DAY 7—WALK WITHOUT HEADPHONES.

Let your mind wander. What thought keeps coming back? That might be your whisper.

_____

_____

_____

_____

_____

WEEK 2: BUILD THE SYSTEM

Goal: Create structure that frees you and makes real progress visible.

DAY 8—CHOOSE A DAILY NONNEGOTIABLE.

Pick one thing (journaling, walking, writing, deep work) and commit for seven days.

DAY 9—PICK A PLATFORM.

Choose one content platform (email, podcast, YouTube, blog). This is your base.

DAY 10—BUILD A ONE-LINER.

Write a sentence that explains who you help, with what, and how you're different (this is your mission).

_____

_____

_____

_____

_____

DAY 11—SKETCH YOUR FIRST OFFER.

Free or paid. What's something small but valuable you can offer?

_____

_____

_____

_____

DAY 12—CREATE BEFORE YOU CONSUME.

Don't touch your phone in the morning until you've created something.

DAY 13—BUILD YOUR FU BUDGET

List three things you can cut and one recurring income idea you could add.

1. _____
2. _____
3. _____

1. _____

DAY 14—SET UP A WEEKLY REVIEW BLOCK.

Block 30 minutes on your calendar every Sunday to ask: "What's working? What's not?"

_____
_____
_____
_____
_____

WEEK 3: GROW THE FREEDOM

Goal: Scale momentum. Serve with purpose. Stay in the game.

DAY 15—CREATE SOMETHING SMALL.

Write one email. Record a three-minute video. Build momentum through action.

DAY 16—REACH OUT TO ONE PERSON.

A mentor. A peer. A connector. Send a thank you or request a 15-minute call.

DAY 17—DO A 30-MINUTE DIGITAL DETOX.

Go completely offline. No phone. No laptop. Just be.

DAY 18—TEACH SOMETHING PUBLICLY.

Share a lesson, framework, or story online. Don't overthink it. Publish it.

DAY 19—REVISIT YOUR TILT.

Has it shifted? Clarify or sharpen it based on what you've learned.

_____

_____

_____

_____

_____

DAY 20—WRITE YOUR NEW 90-DAY VISION.

What do you want to have created, built, or launched in three months?

_____

_____

_____

_____

_____

DAY 21—COMMIT TO ONE TINY HABIT.

Choose one action you'll keep doing daily for the next 30 days.

_____

_____

_____

_____

_____

APPENDIX A

THE CONTENT INC. MODEL

In 2007, I left my comfortable six-figure job with no product, no audience, and little money in the bank. What I did have was a belief that if I could build an audience first . . . by consistently delivering helpful, focused content . . . then I could build a business on the back of that trust.

That idea became the Content Inc. model, which I've since written about, taught, and personally lived through multiple successful ventures.

At its heart, Content Inc. flips the traditional business model. Instead of creating a product first and then trying to find customers, it starts with content . . . building an audience around a clear niche and then identifying what they want to buy.

It's the ultimate "Build once. Sell forever" system.

Here's a high-level overview of the seven steps of the model:

1. **The sweet spot.** Find the intersection of what you're passionate about or skilled in and what a specific audience cares about. This isn't about being everything to everyone. It's about being

uniquely valuable to someone.

2. **Content Tilt.** Your Tilt is what separates you from everyone else creating similar content. It's the angle, voice, or worldview that makes your content stand out. Without a Tilt, you're just more noise.

3. **Build the base.** Pick one content type (audio, video, or written), pick one platform (podcast, YouTube, blog, etc.), and publish consistently. Most people fail here because they try to do too much too soon. Do one thing great.

4. **Build an audience.** Move from rented platforms (like social media) to owned platforms (like email). Email subscribers are the gold standard. They're how you turn casual readers into a loyal tribe.

5. **Revenue.** Once you've built trust and attention, revenue opportunities will emerge: digital products, memberships, books, consulting, sponsorships, events, or physical products. Many Content Inc. creators monetize in five to seven ways at once.

6. **Diversify.** Only after you have a loyal audience should you expand to new content types or platforms. Build a strong core first; then branch out . . . just like ESPN started with one cable channel and slowly expanded.

7. **Sell or go big.** Eventually, you'll hit a decision point: Sell the business and walk away with financial freedom, or scale up into a larger enterprise. Either path can lead to the "FU position" this book advocates.

WHY THIS SECTION BELONGS IN THIS BOOK

This book is about building a life on your terms. One rooted in ownership, trust, and time freedom. Content Inc. is one of the most powerful and practical frameworks I know for making that real. It doesn't matter if you're a teacher, gamer, photographer, writer, consultant, or engineer. If you can build an audience, you can build a business.

And once you've built it? You'll never need a résumé again.

APPENDIX B

MY RESOURCE LIST

Throughout *Burn the Playbook*, I've referenced a number of books and resources that shaped how I think about business, content creation, wealth, and personal freedom. Some were quoted directly. Others simply shifted how I live and work.

This isn't a ranked resource list. It's a curated resource list. If you're serious about building something that lasts, on your terms, this is a great place to start.

Books That Influenced *Burn the Playbook*

- *Think and Grow Rich* by Napoleon Hill. The foundation for goal setting, belief, and achievement . . . revisited and challenged throughout this book. *Burn the Playbook* would not exist without *Think and Grow Rich*.

- *Atomic Habits* by James Clear. A system I've found for building identity-based habits that actually stick.

- *The 7 Habits of Highly Effective People* by Stephen R. Covey. Timeless principles for aligning your actions with your values. A book I return to often.

- *They Ask, You Answer* by Marcus Sheridan. A no-BS blueprint for building trust through honest, transparent content.

- *Superfans* by Pat Flynn. Shows how to grow an audience that buys from you because they believe in you.

- *Stand the F*ck Out* by Louis Grenier. A punch-in-the-gut reminder that playing it safe is a great way to be invisible.

- *The Psychology of Money* by Morgan Housel. Brilliant and simple insights on how your mindset, not your math, determines your financial freedom.

- *The Five Types of Wealth* by Sahil Bloom. Helps you to rethink what wealth really means for you. Hint: It's different for everyone.

- *Stranger in a Strange Land* by Robert A. Heinlein. A fictional but deeply philosophical exploration of belief, individuality, and culture.

Books That Shaped My Content Philosophy

- *Everybody Writes* by Ann Handley. If you're writing for an audience, this is your style guide, coach, and tough-love editor in one.

- *Brandscaping* by Andrew Davis. A powerful strategy book on how to grow your brand by creating content partnerships instead of ads.

- *Youtility* by Jay Baer. A practical guide to building loyalty by being incredibly useful.

- *Marketing Rebellion* by Mark Schaefer. A human-first take on how modern marketing must evolve or die.

- *The New Rules of Marketing & PR* by David Meerman Scott. One of the earliest books to explain why publishing your own content is the future (and it still is).

- *Blue Ocean Strategy* by W. Chan Kim and Renée Mauborgne. Stop fighting over scraps. Create something entirely new and uncontested.

- *Jab, Jab, Jab, Right Hook* by Gary Vaynerchuk. A tactical reminder that value should lead before the ask.

- *Sponsor Magnet* by Justin Moore. *The* guide on finding brand partnerships to fuel your content business.

- *Experiences: The 7th Era of Marketing* by Robert Rose and Carla Johnson. A brilliant framework for creating content that behaves like a product and builds trust over time.

- *IMC: The Next Generation* by Don Schultz and Heidi Schultz. Don was one of my mentors. He taught me so much, and this book is a great primer for understanding communication.

- *Duct Tape Marketing* by John Jantsch. Written over a decade ago, this book still packs a punch for understanding sales and content (plus it's been updated).

- *Epic Content Marketing* by Joe Pulizzi and Brian Piper. The playbook that helped start the global content marketing movement.

Books on Health, Focus, and Longevity

- *Outlive* by Peter Attia. A masterclass in how to think about lifespan and healthspan. Required reading.

- *Super Agers* by Eric Topol. A thorough guide to living longer and better.

- *Why We Sleep* by Matthew Walker. Deeply influenced how I think about productivity, creativity, and energy.

- *The Comfort Crisis* by Michael Easter. Reminds us why discomfort is often the path to growth, resilience, and real freedom.

- *The End of Alzheimer's* by Dale Bredesen. A practical, science-backed guide to protecting your brain health as you pursue a longer, more purposeful life.

Resources I Rely On

- **Morning Brew.** News digest that helps me find important news.
- **Creator Science** by Jay Clouse. Jay is the real deal, and his advice is second to none.
- *Andy Crestodina's Newsletter.* Want to be found on the internet? Andy will help.
- *Simon Owens's Media Newsletter.* Incredible insight into what small creators and media companies are doing.
- **They Got Acquired** by Lexi Grant. How small creators are exiting their businesses and winning.
- *Diary of a CEO Podcast* by Stephen Bartlett. Incredible guests, many of whom helped inspire this book.
- *The Prof G* Pod by Scott Galloway. A must listen every Thursday.
- **Rand Fishkin.** Rand posts regular video updates on the latest in findability on his LinkedIn page. Worth the follow.
- *The Artificial Intelligence Podcast* with Paul Roetzer and Mike Kaput. No better source for the latest in AI.
- *The Saturday Solopreneur newsletter* by Justin Welsh. Always something useful for entrepreneurs each week.

These resources reflect the philosophy behind *Burn the Playbook* . . . ownership, courage, clarity, and focus.

If you read or listen to even a handful, take notes, and actually apply what you learn . . . you'll be way ahead of the crowd still waiting for permission.

APPENDIX C

"TAKING THE LEAP" WORKSHEET

Plan the exit. Don't wing it.

1. **Define your why.** Why are you making this leap? What are you walking away from, and what are you walking toward?

I want to leave my current job because . . .

_____

_____

_____

_____

_____

What I truly want to build is . . .

_____

_____

_____

_____

_____

2. **Calculate your baseline freedom number.** What's the _minimum_ monthly income you need to cover your essentials?

Expense Category	Monthly Cost
Rent/Mortgage	$_____
Utilities/Internet	$_____
Food/Groceries	$_____
Insurance (health, car)	$_____
Debt Payments	$_____
Transportation	$_____
Misc. Essentials	$_____

TOTAL minimum monthly income needed: $_____

Now multiply by 3 or 6 (runway months):

Ideal runway savings: $_____

3. **Audit your skills and systems.** What are you building now that can become a real income stream?

My Tilt: _____

Audience I serve: _____

Platform I create on: _____

First offer (or future offer): _____

Monetization method (e.g., course, coaching, product):

_____

_____

_____

_____

_____

4. Prep Your People

Who needs to be looped in or considered before you leap?

Supporters to inform:

_____

_____

_____

_____

_____

Difficult conversations to plan:

_____

_____

_____

_____

Trusted advisors/mentors to consult:

_____

_____

_____

_____

_____

5. **Pick your go date.** Choose a realistic but challenging timeline for when you'll transition.

Go date (target quit date/shift to full-time creator): _____

Work backward:

- When will you start reducing hours or consulting instead of working full-time?
- What's your content/promotion schedule leading up to it?
- What needs to be automated or delegated?

6. **Commit to the first three moves.** Momentum wins. List your next small steps:

1. _____

2. _____

3. _____

FINAL REMINDER

This won't be perfect. It won't be linear.

But it will be worth it.

Print this. Revisit it. Adjust it. Act on it.

The plan is the bridge. The leap is still yours to take.

APPENDIX D

RESOURCES BY CHAPTER

Below is a chapter-by-chapter reference list of resources, links, and citations mentioned throughout *Burn the Playbook*. These will help you dig deeper, explore supporting studies, and follow the trail of insights that shaped this book.

Chapter 1: The Dream Was a Lie

- Federal Reserve college graduation debt—https://educationdata. org/average-student-loan-debt
- Economic Policy Institute income stagnation—https://www.epi. org/publication/swa-wages-2019/
- Pew Research economic outlook—https://www.pewresearch.org/ politics/2025/04/23/economic-ratings-and-concerns-2025/
- TIAA retirement data—https://www.tiaa.org/public/ investment-performance
- National Alliance to End Homelessness—https://endhomeless-ness.org/
- The Annie E. Casey Foundation—https://www.aecf.org/

- The Title Report on fewer Americans owning homes—https://www.thetitlereport.com/articles/redfin-fewer-young-americans-own-homes-94025.aspx

- World Health Organization anxiety and depression—https://www.who.int/news/item/02-03-2022-covid-19-pandemic-triggers-25-increase-in-prevalence-of-anxiety-and-depression-worldwide

- *Time* on why everyone is having bad sex—https://time.com/6283422/bad-sex-young-people/

- American Psychiatric Association, "New APA Poll: One in Three Americans Feels Lonely Every Week"—https://www.psychiatry.org/news-room/news-releases/new-apa-poll-one-in-three-americans-feels-lonely-e

- American Academy of Pediatrics national emergency—https://www.aap.org/en/advocacy/child-and-adolescent-healthy-mental-development/aap-aacap-cha-declaration-of-a-national-emergency-in-child-and-adolescent-mental-health/

- Steve Jobs's "Think Different" speech—https://www.youtube.com/watch?v=b4n8uT12ij8

Chapter 2: Belief over Proof

- Tilt Creator Economy Benchmark study—https://www.thetilt.com/research

- Edelman Trust Barometer—https://www.edelman.com/trust/trust-barometer

- U.S. SBA business stats—https://data.sba.gov/

- Dr. Tara Swart on belief rewiring—https://www.taraswart.com/

- Gallup poll on goal setting—https://news.gallup.com/poll/467696/seven-americans-likely-set-goals-2023.aspx

- Dr. Rozen personal goal study—https://www.drmichellerozen. com/goal-setting/6-percent-research/

Chapter 3: You Are What You Repeat

- Duke University habit study—https://today.duke.edu/2016/01/ habits

- Tilt Creator Economy Benchmark study—https://www.thetilt. com/research

- ScienceDirect on music repetition—https://www.sciencedirect. com/science/article/abs/pii/S1057740814001260

- UC Irvine multitasking study—https://news.uci.edu/2020/04/19/ why-attention-management-is-the-secret-sauce-to-success-du- ring-the-pandemic-and-after/

Chapter 4: Expertise Beats Credentials

- LinkedIn Future of Work report—https://economicgraph. linkedin.com/research/future-of-work-report-ai

- Substack for paid newsletters—https://substack.com/going-paid

- Patreon for creators – https://www.patreon.com/pricing

Chapter 5: Create Like an Artist. Sell Like a Pro

- Amanda Palmer TED Talk: "The Art of Asking"—https://www. ted.com/talks/amanda_palmer_the_art_of_asking?language=en

Chapter 6: Focus Is Freedom

- ConvertKit Creator Survey—https://convertkit.com/reports/ creator-economy-2023

- Marie Forleo's B-School—https://www.marieforleo.com/

Chapter 7: Build Once. Sell Forever

- ConvertKit Creator Survey—https://convertkit.com/reports/creator-economy-2023

- Tilt Study on creators—https://www.thetilt.com/research

- River Pools & Spas case study—https://www.hubspot.com/customers/river-pools

- Business Insider MrBeast Revenue—https://www.businessinsider.com/mrbeast-business-breakdown-revenue-streams-2024

Chapter 8: The Algorithm Is Patience

- Tilt Study on creators—https://www.thetilt.com/research

- Hubspot State of Blogging Report—https://blog.hubspot.com/marketing/state-of-blogging

Chapter 9: Curate Your Crew

- Harvard Study on personal networks—https://hbr.org/2007/01/how-leaders-create-and-use-networks

- SCORE Foundation—https://www.score.org/

- Founder Reports on anxiety—https://founderreports.com/entrepreneur-mental-health-statistics/

Chapter 10: The Undiscovered Countries

Older Adults (The "Silver Tsunami")

- U.S. Census Bureau demographic shift (2034 projection)—https://www.census.gov/library/publications/2020/demo/p25-1144.html

- AT&T commitment to digital equity and seniors—https://about.att.com/story/2024/digital-divide-recommitment.html

- Digital literacy initiative for older adults—https://www.attconnects.com/improving-digital-literacy-for-all-ages/

New Entrepreneurs and Side Hustlers

- Record-breaking 5.5 million new business applications (2023)—https://www.uschamber.com/small-business/new-business-applications-a-state-by-state-view

- 42 percent of start-ups fail due to no market need—https://www.failory.com/startups/no-market-need-failures

- 82 percent of small businesses fail due to cash flow issues—https://www.score.org/resource/blog-post/1-reason-small-businesses-fail-and-how-avoid-it

Small B2B and Industrial Businesses

- 98 percent of U.S. manufacturers have fewer than 100 employees—https://www.linkedin.com/posts/nishchaldua_98-of-registered-companies-in-the-us-have-activity-7191718059496165376-4iuv

- Only 19 percent of B2B companies effectively use AI—https://www.linkedin.com/pulse/why-most-b2b-companies-get-ai-wrong-how-fix-darius-grigaliunas-13clf

- Technology can increase margins by up to 60 percent—https://moldstud.com/articles/p-boosting-productivity-how-a-technology-company-enhanced-efficiency-with-bi-solutions

Emerging Tech Users

- 63 percent of Americans don't trust cryptocurrency safety—https://www.icba.org/newsroom/news-and-articles/2024/10/29/pew-research-americans-don-t-think-crypto-is-safe

- ChatGPT reached 100 million users in 2 months—https://www.reuters.com/technology/chatgpt-sets-record-fastest-growing-user-base-analyst-note-2023-02-01/

Rural and Remote Communities

- 60 million Americans live in rural areas—https://www.census.gov/library/stories/2017/08/rural-america.html

- 22.3 percent of rural Americans lack broadband access—https://www.usda.gov/sustainability/infrastructure/broadband

- 700+ rural hospitals at risk of closing—https://www.healthcaredive.com/news/hundreds-rural-hospitals-risk-closing-center-healthcare-quality-payment-reform/723555/

- Over 200 counties with no local newspaper—https://www.usnewsdeserts.com/reports/expanding-news-desert/loss-of-local-news/

Chapter 11: Your FU Financial Position

- *The Gambler* (2014) starring Mark Wahlberg

- Bureau of Labor Statistics—https://www.bls.gov/

- Roth IRA basics—https://www.investopedia.com/terms/r/rothira.asp

Chapter 12: Protect Your Feed

- *PCMag* phone time—https://www.pcmag.com/news/americans-check-their-phones-an-alarming-number-of-times-per-day

- Cal Newport—https://www.calnewport.com/

Chapter 13: Stay Healthy to Stay Free

- Bredesen, Dale. *The End of Alzheimer's*. Penguin, 2017.—https://www.drbredesen.com/

- Attia, Dr. Peter. *Outlive*. Harmony/Rodale/Convergent, 2023.—https://www.peterattiamd.com/

- Topol, Eric. *Super Agers*. Simon & Schuster, 2025.—https://www.simonandschuster.com/books/Super-Agers/Eric-Topol/9781668067666

- Autophagy and Dr. Yoshinori Ohsumi's Nobel Prize—https://www.nobelprize.org/prizes/medicine/2016/ohsumi/facts/

Chapter 14: Upgrade Your Mental Operating System

- Carol Dweck on growth mindset—https://www.mindsetworks.com/

- Fogg, BJ. *Tiny Habits*. Houghton Mifflin Harcourt, 2019.—https://www.tinyhabits.com/

- Jay Shetty—https://jayshetty.me/

Chapter 15: Listen to the Whisper

- *Harvard Business Review* on unstructured thinking—https://hbr.org/2002/08/creativity-under-the-gun

- Iowa Gambling Task—https://en.wikipedia.org/wiki/Iowa_gambling_task

Chapter 16: Build the System That Frees You

- USC study on routines—https://www.psychologytoday.com/us/blog/the-athletes-way/201305/the-secret-to-achieving-a-big-goal-is

ACKNOWLEDGMENTS

The Firestarters

This book exists because a handful of people fanned the flame before I knew exactly what I was building.

To **Jim McDermott**, who introduced me to Brian Tracy, goal setting, and content marketing. It makes me smile that you would love this book the most.

To the **Tilt Publishing**, **CEX**, and **Lulu** teams and the **CEX VIP community**, who walk the talk every day. This book is stitched together from your stories, wins, scars, and questions.

To the first reviewers of this book. Your input was invaluable. Especially **Jim Kukral**, **Brian Piper**, and **David Heath**.

To **Robert Rose, Andrew Davis, David Nussbaum, Ann Handley, Don Pazour, Jeff Forker, Gary Kelley, Diana Pohly, Angela Vannucci, Scott Owen, Dr. Dan Canary, F. Leo Groff, Charles Meyst, Karen Horacek, Lee Zapis, Paul Roetzer, Kelley Whetsell, JK Kalinowski, Jesse Cole, Marc Maxhimer, Bill Donahue, Peter Loibl, Cathy McPhillips, Michele Linn, Clare McDermott, Laura Kozak, Leon Groff, Ed Kozelka, Gus Castallanos, Matt Briel, Michael Paul, Jeremy Smith, Dave Anthony, Jay Baer, Peter Kwiatkowski, Nick Offerman, Newt Barrett, Jane Battes, Brian Clark, Greg Watt, Chris Van Gils, Lee**

Zapis, Ann Gynn, Michelle Martello, Marco Pardi, Paul Wadsworth, Lynn Cole, Lou Grasso, Kevin Lednik, Peter Hoyt, and so many others.

To my **newsletter readers and podcast listeners,** especially those who hit reply or sent a note at just the right moment. You reminded me that this work matters.

To the **Tipsy Ten,** who continue to partake in crazy experiences with me, even when I may not know exactly what is going on.

To **my children,** who make me think harder about what legacy really means. Keep being amazing.

To **Pam,** who always sees the next version of me before I do and loves me through the chaos of getting there. You are the constant in the creation.

And to you holding this book: If even one line helped you see a way forward, I hope you underline it, copy it, post it, or whisper it to a friend. That's how we burn the playbook…together.

Let's go build something that matters.

Let's go set fires.

ABOUT JOE PULIZZI

Joe Pulizzi is an entrepreneur, speaker, author, and one of the founders of the content marketing movement. He's the creator of the Content Inc. model, founder of multiple successful businesses (The Tilt, Content Marketing Institute), and author of eight books, including *Content Inc.*, *Epic Content Marketing*, and the thriller novel *The Will to Die*. Joe is also the creator of Content Entrepreneur Expo (CEX) and Content Marketing World, the largest physical content marketing event in the world. He lives in Cleveland, Ohio, with his wife and two children and believes the ultimate freedom comes from building something you own.

Want more Joe? Get his bimonthly newsletter at JoePulizzi.com.

Joe recommends these books:

The Content Entrepreneur

Don't be a content creator. Be t*he* content entrepreneur.

Business-changing insights from 33 experts on the proven way to build a content business.

In this comprehensive guide for serious content creators, you'll find critical strategies to accelerate your success as you move from content creator to content entrepreneur.

The Will to Die

The Will to Die is a shocking small-town murder mystery starring marketing professional Will Pollitt. It was awarded the "Best Suspense Book" by the National Indie Excellence Awards. BestThrillers.com called it a "top-shelf crime thriller."

Epic Content Marketing

Now in its second edition (2023), *Epic Content Marketing* is generally regarded as the most popular and comprehensive book on the practice of content marketing. It's required reading for any marketing professional, especially those involved in corporate content creation or distribution.

Epic Content Marketing has sold more than 100,000 copies worldwide and has been translated into dozens of languages.

Content Inc.

Content Inc. is the business model for content creators. In other words, if you want to become a content entrepreneur, *Content Inc.* will tell you how in seven steps. This is the model I've used myself to sell three content-based companies for millions of dollars.

Get more at https://www.joepulizzi.com/books/.